GARDENING *in* MINIATURE

*To Steve, the other pea in my pod*

Published in 2013 by Timber Press, Inc.

The Haseltine Building
133 S.W. Second Avenue, Suite 450       6a Lonsdale Road
Portland, Oregon 97204-3527             London NW6 6RD
timberpress.com                         timberpress.co.uk

Printed in China
Second printing 2013

Book design by Laken Wright

Library of Congress Cataloging-in-Publication Data

Calvo, Janit.
  Gardening in miniature : create your own tiny living world/Janit Calvo;
with photographs by Kate Baldwin.—1st ed.
     p. cm.
  Includes bibliographical references and index.
  ISBN 978-1-60469-372-0
1. Gardens, Miniature. 2. Miniature plants. I. Baldwin, Kate. II. Title.
  SB433.5.C37123 2013
  635.9—dc23                              2012041271

A catalog record for this book is also available from the British Library.

# GARDENING *in* MINIATURE

JANIT CALVO

*Create Your Own Tiny*
*Living World*

with photographs by
KATE BALDWIN

**TIMBER PRESS**
PORTLAND | LONDON

# Contents

8

*Good Things Come in Small Gardens*
## AN INTRODUCTION

20

*Do a Little Gardening*
## MINIATURE WORLDS 101

108

*It Needs You, You Need It*
## GARDEN CARE

138

*Personality Plus*
## MINIATURE GARDEN ACCESSORIES

# PREFACE

I HAVE WITNESSED many people jump up and down, clap their hands, and squeal with excitement—all simultaneously—after seeing their first miniature garden. I've also had people write me long e-mails about their first garden, curse me (jokingly) for getting them started, and even phone to thank me for introducing them to this captivating hobby. I tell them if miniature gardening wasn't so much fun, I wouldn't be doing it.

Over the years, the concept has gradually caught on and been embraced throughout the world. Some seem to think it's child's play and not for real gardeners, but if they pick up this book and read it, they will find that gardening in miniature can be as challenging as designing a full-sized garden; proportion and scale, elements of garden design, and sustainability all need to be considered.

It is a great way to get kids into the garden, but people are often surprised to learn that most miniature gardeners are over forty-five years old.

It was a natural progression for me to write a book on the subject. I'm a publisher's daughter who was born and bred into the hobby and collectibles industry in Toronto. My family's press is dedicated to cataloging many collecting hobbies—coins, hockey cards, and Royal Doulton figurines, just to name a few. So the instinct to gather new information on this hobby was ingrained. Once I found out that miniature gardening had yet to be updated and fully explored, I knew I had to dig deeper—a lot deeper. When I discovered that a book like this didn't exist, I looked around to find other experts with the experience and knowledge that I had accumulated, only to find none. I knew then that I was the one who had to write this book.

The information shared here comes from more than twelve years of working full-time promoting this hobby throughout the United States, Canada, and the world. Some of my miniature gardens have been with me for over nine years and are still thriving—a testament to the longevity and sustainability of miniature gardening. And a number of my customers, my beloved fellow miniature gardeners (MGs), have been with me for just as long—proof of the depth and breadth of this hobby.

I know you will enjoy this book as much as I enjoyed putting it together for you. The introduction will start your gears turning with an overview of the many facets of this delightful pastime. Next up is a look at the basics of miniature gardening and its elements, both the physical and the intangible, followed by a chapter on scale and sizing. A look at tiny patios and pathways—key components of most miniature gardens—comes next. A quick tour of the land of miniature plants follows, including details on growth habits and how to best use specific plants, as well as a brief list of plant recommendations. These suggestions merely scratch the surface; the number of miniature plants available grows exponentially as I write this. Next is a chapter full of the basics of soil, light, and watering—all especially helpful for new gardeners. A chapter on garden accessories offers tips on adding personality and realism. Then, the really fun stuff: hands-on, how-to projects large and small, to guide you through how I make my long-lasting miniature gardens. You'll find lakes, riverbeds, and ponds in there along with some handmade garden accessory ideas. We finish up with all-important instructions on maintaining healthy, thriving miniature gardens. I've also included some additional reading suggestions for those whose curiosity has been piqued.

For most of us, anything miniature brings to mind the days when we were young and full of imagination, spinning tales of majesty and grandeur. The garden brings us beauty and lovely living things to nurture and grow. Together they create something magical, yet just challenging enough to hold our interest from year to year. You can build a miniature garden in an afternoon, or it can take several stages to achieve your goal. There is no right or wrong way, only your way. Best of all, it's your world to grow, so remember: whatever you do, make it fun.

## GOOD THINGS COME
## IN SMALL GARDENS
### AN INTRODUCTION

WHAT IS IT THAT draws the heart and eye to things smaller than real life? Perhaps the fact that anything miniature reminds us of play. After all, our childhood toys were our first miniatures. Whether they were Lincoln Logs, Legos, Barbies, G.I. Joes, or other kinds of dolls, our toys were always miniature versions of us or other parts of our lives. We projected ourselves into the scene and got lost in the small version of our world, exactly how we liked it. Those positive feelings of play and laughter were—and still are—vital to our happiness, and when we see miniatures and remember our fun, carefree playtimes, we feel that way again.

*A life-sized bridge to cross, or miniature to admire? Illusion can be enchanting.*

The sense of wonder that comes over us can be quite potent. When you are the writer and director, creating the story, setting the scene, and placing the props, you bring that innocent pleasure into your adult life under the guise of a hobby. But really, hobbies just give us permission to play again.

Many miniaturists are enamored with the idea of anything small because miniatures are a part of our history. The oldest known human artifact is a diminutive replica of the female form, the Venus of Hohle Fels, dated between 35,000 and 40,000 B.C. This tiny sculpture is just under two and a half inches tall. Dollhouse miniature themes are often a memory from childhood, a place visited in the past, or a love of a specific historical period. It is noteworthy that the main themes of dollhouse miniatures and model railroads are historical, reminding us of a simpler time. Model or garden railroading takes us on a journey through a specific landscape that is either a historical model, or comes from the creator's mind. You can't help but imagine yourself in the scene.

This passion for miniatures has found its way into other aspects of our lives as well. Live, miniature-sized horses and dogs have long been popular; now you can own miniature cows and goats, too. Then there was the fleeting fad of teacup (tiny) pigs a few years ago. It turned out they were just very young piglets, being sold as a miniature breed. Fantasy games are full of pint-sized versions of characters that players collect. The horticultural industry has kept up with this interest as well, breeding tiny vegetables that can easily be grown from seed. Dwarf and miniature forms of our favorite trees, shrubs, and perennials have been discovered over the last few decades and are now found in most garden centers.

*Flowers in the maiden's hands match nearby miniature daisies.*

*Make a place for pets in your garden scenes.*

LEFT: *This charming oasis invites visitors to rest a spell.*

RIGHT: *Woodland creatures nestled into the scene add focus.*

From that initial spark comes the challenge of figuring out how to perfect the illusion—resizing from big to small in flawless scale, hunting for and utilizing believable materials, mastering techniques that will both trick and delight the eye. The end reward is seeing a face light up when the viewer experiences the sprinkling of magic that infuses a lovingly made miniature scene.

A miniature garden scene is enchanting because you automatically start building a story about it. You ask yourself, what's going on here? Who are those chairs for? What kind of party is that little table set for? Are there friends or family coming over? What is the occasion? The imagination starts to fill in the blanks as props lend clues and personality. A tiny stool with a watering can beside it, placed in a small miniature garden vignette, is intriguing because it's only a scene with no characters—who could it be for besides you?

Gardening is part of our collective psyche even more than our fascination with miniaturization. To blend both—creating gardens in miniature, with living trees, shrubs, bedding plants, water features, furniture, and garden art—is to open up limitless

LEFT: *Fill miniature planters with sedum cuttings that will eventually take root.*

RIGHT: *A cozy spot for a warm fire. S'mores, anyone?*

possibilities for bringing dreamscapes, wonderlands, and enchanting places from our past or our imaginations to vibrant life, in no small way.

Once you are bitten by the miniature garden bug, there is no turning back. The possibilities will start to stack up in your head at all hours of the day and night, and there is often a squeal of excitement involved somewhere in this process (it's okay, just let it out when it happens and explain yourself later—but only if you have to). Do you dream of recreating that garden memory of your year spent in Europe? A vignette taken from your childhood growing up on your grandmother's farm? Maybe you've always wanted your own garden oasis but you live in a condo. Now is the time to dream and scheme!

ABOVE: *Complex scenes engage and intrigue.*

BELOW: *This haven is no less beautiful than its full-sized counterpart.*

RIGHT: *Natural treasures delight in unexpected places.*

*A full-sized backyard walkway?*
*Or a tiny garden path?*

*A whimsical find for the keen eye.*

## DO A LITTLE GARDENING
MINIATURE WORLDS 101

MINIATURE GARDENING is that sweet spot where craft and gardening intersect at such an intimately creative place; it can spur your imagination like no other hobby. Best of all, you can bring the garden of your dreams to life in one afternoon, sitting at your kitchen table. What a satisfying way to plant, grow, and create—without breaking your back or your bank account!

*Darkened doorways add intrigue. Who lives there? What's on the other side?*

Gardening in miniature takes many forms—the term "miniature garden" used to mean any small-sized plant in a small pot. Terrariums, bonsai, dish gardens, and windowsill gardens all fit under the umbrella of miniature gardens simply because of their size. A collection of African violets on a windowsill is just that, a collection—often only appreciated by the collector or a fellow plant lover. But place a small potted plant on a windowsill, put a miniature chair and a tiny watering can beside it, and suddenly you have a story to tell that anyone, from age four to one hundred and four, can interpret for themselves. Place a miniature garden bench in a terrarium, sprinkle some micro pebbles down at the base of the bench for an impromptu patio, and you have just made a miniature garden terrarium. It can be as simple as that. But a miniature garden can also have many layers and even more possibilities, without needing to be a terrarium, a bonsai, or a dish garden first.

A miniature garden is as real as a full-sized garden, with living trees and plants, patios, pathways, and garden furniture, but everything is on a much smaller scale—and in scale with everything else in the miniature garden. It can fit into a pot as small as two inches wide, or into a parking strip twenty feet long by six feet wide. Miniature gardening is about your own world, so you can make it as big or as small as you like.

When you start to break down the components of a miniature garden, you'll find the options keep multiplying. The sheer number of possible trees, plants, pots, themes, and accessories starts to grow and the idea can become a bit daunting. Stop and think of a full-sized garden. You'll begin to see the entry points with which you're already familiar—you just have to miniaturize them now. Almost all of the same garden rules apply, but with a little miniaturist insight, a slight twist to basic artistic rules, and ideas on how to see things differently as a designer and inventor, I will show you how to create an unexpected world-within-a-world of your very own.

*Tiny container gardens can be created in a few minutes.*

*"Go over the bridge and down the path."*

# START GROWING YOUR OWN WORLD

Miniature gardening will get your creative juices flowing so rapidly at first, you won't know where to begin. Do you start with the plants or the pot? What about the miniature furniture? How big should it be? One of the first questions you have to ask is where is your miniature garden going to live? Deciding where—and in what—your miniature garden will be planted immediately narrows down other choices.

Your available space will probably play a role in the size of your garden. If you are new to the hobby, a garden in a container (rather than inground outdoors) is less intimidating, easier to care for, and a faster project to complete with very satisfying results. Container gardening is a little different from growing inground because you become the source for water, nourishment, and care. An inground miniature garden will eventually establish itself and, for the most part, become low maintenance because plant roots will find their own food and water.

Will you create your miniature garden in a tall, skinny pot by the front door to welcome your guests? It would be a terrific spot to decorate for the holidays and special occasions. Imagine the smiles you could generate if the quaint garden scene was a replica of your full-sized front garden. Placing your miniature garden in a prominent place where it can be readily seen and appreciated is a

ABOVE: *A bonsai pot is turned into a miniature koi pond.*

BELOW: *A ladybug is the perfect pet for a tiny cherub.*

great way to interact with others. Just the thought of decorating for your Halloween party with a little pumpkin, a black cat, and a wee gravestone is in itself a great reason to build a miniature garden—not to mention watching your guests laugh before they even step into your party.

Indoor miniature gardens can vary greatly. A low bowl planted with a garden in the round (so that it can be viewed from all sides) and placed on a table is an unusual centerpiece and a great conversation starter. You can create a circular path all around the edge of the bowl with a garden bed in the middle of the pot or, vice versa, plant all around the rim of the pot and build a round patio right in

the middle. Use low-growing plants so you can see over the garden to the person across the table and keep the conversation going. Place your tablescape on a Lazy Susan for interactive fun.

Tending a raised planter box in front of a living room window can be the perfect way to spend a sunny morning. A miniature garden can be a large, single-sided Italian garden with a young Monterey cypress, a brick-wall fountain, and a cobblestone plaza with cafe tables and chairs that sits on your credenza. Or, create a tiny garden for your night-stand with a small rooted cutting of a succulent, a birdhouse, and a fence to welcome you to your day and bid you goodnight.

LEFT: *It's easy to keep small-sized gardens as neat as a pin.*

RIGHT: *Holidays such as Halloween are fun themes for miniature scenes.*

## INGROUND EMPIRES

Building a miniature garden in a garden bed can be very rewarding, but some forethought is required. When you plant in a pot, its size dictates the parameters of your miniature garden. When planting inground, you are working with what's already there: shrubs, hedges, flowerbeds, walkways, decks, or patios.

Some perfect places for an inground miniature world are in the corners of existing garden beds, between shrubs, next to a big tree, or in a hidden nook beside a garden gate. Choose a spot you will see often so you can visit your own little world regularly. If you entertain, consider a place that will reward a guest for being observant—for example, at the end of a garden path. You will enjoy seeing who notices and how long it takes them.

*Inground miniature gardens often look identical to full-sized scenes.*

## IT'S IN THE POT

LEFT: *One container can be divided to house two garden beds.*

RIGHT: *From large to tiny, ceramic to wood, there's a container for every style of miniature garden.*

The type of container you'll use for a potted garden will depend upon your tastes, the garden theme, what you are planting, where you live, where the scene is going to be placed, and how experienced you are with container gardening. Remember that your miniature garden, wherever it lives, will last for years and years, if you want it to. So, choosing a pot that will not only wear well but also look great will help you continue to enjoy your garden over time.

If you are in an area that freezes in the winter, and your garden will be outside, it is best to refer to your local garden center for containers; the staff will know what kinds of pots can withstand your weather. In general, for colder regions, the bigger the pot, the better.

Whether you choose to have a matching saucer will depend upon where the container will be placed—note that all saucers will wick moisture despite being glazed. Clear plastic saucers can be relatively indiscreet for condo and apartment decks. Use a bit of moss to hide the plastic if it is bothersome. If you need to corral water, a good trick is to raise your pots up slightly on pot feet or low stands and hide the clear saucer underneath, centered below the pot's drainage holes.

The size of pot can vary greatly, too. A pot that is four inches deep and wide with a small-leaved sedum and a pint-sized patio can last for a couple of years before needing to be repotted. A small pot tends to dry out rapidly, though, so it should live in a place where it will be seen and cared for.

A favorite container for miniature gardening is a twenty-two-inch water bowl, one foot deep, drilled for drainage. Some nurseries can do this for you, or, with a masonry bit for your drill and a steady trickle of water to keep the bit cool, you can drill it yourself (follow precautions for drilling noted in the tool's instructions). Big bowls can be easily divided into a double-sided miniature garden, with completely different scenes on either side—they can grow together for years if you don't initially overplant.

For a small, starter garden, a pot that is eight to ten inches wide and at least eight inches deep is a great place to begin. Plant it with a tree and a couple of well-behaved bedding plants and it should be able to last for years with regular care and watering.

# POPULAR
# CONTAINER OPTIONS

Any container can be used for a miniature garden, but certain choices are better than others. Pots are available in a number of materials. Aesthetics, watering considerations, cost, and the compatibility of plants with pot materials can all contribute to your decision. There is also a whole category of new containers, made from recycled materials, that are lightweight and weatherproof. Some are made to resemble heavier materials (stone and concrete, for example), and look like the real thing.

Each material has its pros and cons; consider these carefully to make sure you choose the best pot for your needs and situation.

**TERRACOTTA** Unglazed clay or terracotta containers have a natural, homey appearance that no other pots can match. They can look shabby-chic with a white, scuffed finish. Bright paints suggest a contemporary or folksy style. Weathered and mossy finishes lend a French Provincial effect. Whatever the motif, terracotta pots look great lined up on a shelf or down a set of stairs.

Note that miniature gardens planted in terracotta pots will need more frequent watering than those in glazed containers. Terracotta clay is porous and wicks water from the soil and plant roots to the walls of the pot, where it then evaporates in the sun and air. You can move the pot into partial shade or cool (eastern) sun if you want to slow this drying, but make sure the plants you choose can tolerate less sun, too.

If your terracotta garden will be in full sun, choose plants that require less water. Succulents or sedums paired with junipers or mugo pines create a low-maintenance pot.

Terracotta containers are also not for areas that freeze. Because the clay holds water, when that water freezes, the ice expands and can crack the pot.

LEFT: *Plants can help accent patio design.*

CENTER: *Pools and terraces are popular features in miniature container gardens.*

RIGHT: *Terracotta is a favorite choice, but remember that it wicks water from soil and roots.*

LEFT: *A tiny nymph reigns over this indoor garden planted in a glazed porcelain bowl.*

RIGHT: *A deep blue glazed ceramic bowl sets the stage for an inviting outdoor patio scene.*

**CERAMIC** There are multitudes of wonderful colored ceramic containers that are ideal for a miniature garden. Made of clay that is glazed and fired at high temperatures, ceramic pots are not as porous as terracotta and therefore retain water better and are less susceptible to cracking during cold snaps. If you live in an area that freezes during the winter, find the biggest high-fired ceramic pot that you can live with. The bigger the pot, the harder it is to freeze.

Planted, glazed containers dry out slower than unglazed pots. Take advantage of this attribute and choose plants that like a consistent level of dampness in the soil. For example, any dwarf or miniature Alberta spruce needs its roots to stay cool and damp—wrung-sponge damp—because if the soil ever completely dries out, the plant may not recover.

Glazed containers from Vietnam, Thailand, and China are usually high-fired. No single distinction identifies the country of origin, although some of the more decorative pots may have distinctive symbols on them. Containers from these parts of the world are usually fired in huge kilns that leave them susceptible to the odd ding or nick in the glaze. Take a minute when choosing your container to look for these inconsistencies. Nothing is more annoying than getting your pot home and finding an unsightly blemish. Glaze colors are sometimes inconsistent, too. Keep these points in mind when you are shopping.

*A portable wooden container proves you can take it with you.*

**PLASTIC** As with glazed pots, water does not evaporate through the walls of plastic containers, helping them hold moisture longer. However, the UV rays in sunlight can degrade plastic, making the pot susceptible to cracking after a couple of years outside. Color may fade over time, too. An increasing number of plastic containers are coated to resist UV damage—good options if your pot will be moved around a lot and is in regular sunshine. Plastic containers are more lightweight, but be careful when dragging them, as they do get brittle. Instead, pick them up from the bottom for moving. Remember that your miniature world can stay together for years, so the investment in a durable pot is worthwhile.

**WOOD** Wood pots bring a warm, earthy mood to a miniature garden. They are usually inexpensive and lightweight, with many shapes and sizes to choose from. Containers made of cedar, for example, resist rot longer than other woods and are naturally good choices. Placing a wood container on pot feet will help to extend its life by keeping the bottom relatively dry and rot-free.

You can wax, oil, or paint woods to make them last longer, but make sure whatever you do to the inside of the container is plant-friendly. Toxic substances can leach into the soil and plant roots. Likewise, if you are building a wood container from scratch, avoid treated wood, as the chemicals used for the treatment can kill plants.

Wood expands when wet and contracts when dry. There are tiny fibers in the wood that absorb the moisture and swell up, expanding the wood. (This is why your wood kitchen drawers stick in the rainy months.) For this reason, wood wicks moisture away from the soil and can make your garden dry out quickly and sometimes unexpectedly, especially in full-sun conditions.

Choose drought-tolerant plants for wood containers, like a 'Compressa' juniper paired with woolly thyme and 'Cape Blanco' sedum.

*Concrete and stones create
a beautiful surface texture.*

**FAUX STONE** Faux stone pots are great for a themed miniature garden. An embellished stone look can add polish to a wee Italian Renaissance garden full of traditional Roman statues and 'Sky Pencil' Japanese holly—a look-alike miniature for a full-sized Italian cypress.

Faux stone pots made of foam are lightweight but resilient, and will not freeze (though the soil might). The look of stone comes not only from the cast design, but also from how the pot is painted. Despite its tough appearance, though, treat the painted surface gently. It can easily be scratched or nicked to reveal the foam underneath. If foam pots come without drainage holes, you can easily drill them. When they are worn out, you can give them a coat of acrylic paint to lengthen their life. Simple house paint works wonders; just be sure the pot is completely dry and free of dirt before you paint, and leave it to thoroughly dry afterwards.

**HYPERTUFA AND CONCRETE** Hypertufa or concrete containers are perfect for an aged or established look for your miniature garden. Hypertufa is usually a blend of concrete and vermiculite, and is lighter in weight than solid concrete. Containers of solid concrete are great for commercial use or more exposed areas in the front of your property, as they are heavy and unlikely to be stolen. Heavier pots are good for accommodating taller plantings, too. Hypertufa and solid concrete look the same—until you try to pick them up. So if your garden is not to be moved, choose a concrete container.

LEFT: *Tiny inground gardenscapes can be a lovely discovery in the corner of a standard-sized garden.*

RIGHT: *Standard-sized ornamental grasses give this scene an exotic tone.*

## SIZE MATTERS

When you are planting inground, the size of the miniature garden depends on your enthusiasm. Are you willing to spend hours planting and playing while sitting on the ground? If not, go for a smaller, less involved layout. Larger plots are great for children, because you can create enough space for several kids to play in different areas at the same time. Interspersing tiny gardens throughout your yard and linking them together with pathways can be fun. It's also an ongoing project that can be done in stages. Again, try to work with established hedges and plants to help the small-scale garden look like it belongs. A sprawling miniature scene in the middle of the lawn will need context, or something to relate it to the full-sized garden.

Creating a miniature scene between ornamental grasses is a good example of working with existing plantings. You can use the grasses as a backdrop for a tropical island scene. Just add a young variegated English boxwood tree, a pond, and a lounge chair on a bed of fine sand, then sprinkle with tiny shells and small pieces of driftwood. The vertical grass stems will look like bamboo fencing and instantly transport you to a favorite vacation spot.

Planting a miniature garden in front of a rockery can easily suit different themes. Fashion an English garden, with patches of miniature daisies planted along a stone path leading up to a leafy tree. Or plant a country-themed garden with an old wagon wheel sticking out of the ground next to small-leaved sedums, with a few pebbles that match the rockery. By featuring a scaled-down element of the nearby full-sized world, the scene will delight and enchant instantly.

## GETTING A LITTLE GREEN ON

Deciding whether your small-scale garden will be indoors or outdoors, inground or potted, then looking at the light conditions of that chosen spot, will all be key factors in your plant choices. This is why the rule "Right plant, right place" works so well; just because it's a miniature plant doesn't mean it can be grown anywhere, and just because it's in a pot doesn't mean you can place the pot anywhere.

A full-sun plant will not do well in a shady spot and a desert-loving plant will rot in moist soil. An indoor plant will not do well outside unless you live in a place where the temperatures stay above sixty degrees Fahrenheit year-round.

Choosing the correct plants for the place you want to grow your garden makes maintenance easier and helps avoid disappointment. A miniature garden can grow and weave itself together for years before needing a renovation, but only if the plants suit the space.

Also take an honest look at your lifestyle. If you're not home very often or have a busy lifestyle, you'll want plants that don't mind the soil drying out between waterings. If you love doting on plants, look for varieties that thrive in damp soil or with frequent misting. The chapter on miniature garden plants will help you select appropriate plants for all of your needs, but knowing those requirements in the planning stage makes a big difference.

LEFT: *Green fronds shade a reflecting pool.*

RIGHT: *A miniature bucket brigade of hens and chicks brightens a small shelf.*

## SHRINKING THE GARDEN RULES
### SCALED DESIGN BASICS

MINIATURE GARDENING, like any hobby or craft, can be enjoyed at many levels, but the craftsmanship and thought that goes into your creation is what makes it truly captivating. Sure, you can throw any small plant into a pot, add a toy chair, and call it done. Or, you can spend a little time and create a delightful garden that looks like a slice taken out of your full-sized garden, shrunk to miniature size.

*Looks like a sweet celebration is in the works.*

In this chapter, you will learn about the various scales that can be used with success for whatever size miniature scene you are creating. You will also learn full-sized garden rules and how to resize them. The thinking behind the shrinking may take some adjustment, but it is more satisfying to create with the rules than without them. The same full-sized garden design principles apply, too: anchor points, layers, balance, form, texture, color, and focal point—they are just sized down to miniature.

## SIZING DOWN THE SCALES

Your miniature garden design starts with deciding on the size of your container or the spot in your garden bed. Only then can you determine what scale of miniature garden to create. For small gardens, use small plants and accessories, and for large gardens use larger plants and accessories. Sounds simple enough, right? But what does small really mean? And what size is large? Without having a size or scale reference you will not be able to cinch the realism quickly and easily, and the magical element will not happen. You can use the miniature scales we'll discuss as guides to help decide what size garden to create.

Standard-sized home gardens have a single scale: human size. You are the one it's designed for, so you make room for yourself to sit on that antique garden bench at the end of a path that is big enough for you to walk on. The trees and plants fit nicely in your landscape and are not too overwhelming in comparison to the bench and pathway. Everything in your full-sized garden is the same scale, and the sizes of plants, hardscapes, furniture, and any garden accessories are naturally all relative to each other. Now, think about scaling this idea down to a miniature size to create a realistic miniature garden.

LEFT: *The scale in this scene is put into context by the size of the chair.*

RIGHT: *The bench and fire convey scale in this scene.*

# THE SIZE OF MINIATURE

There are many ways to go miniature these days, and just about any scale can be used with success—providing that scale is used consistently throughout the garden. The miniature industry is the biggest segment of the toy and hobby market, and the sheer number of sizes and scales is mind-boggling. Thankfully, in the dollhouse miniature industry we have a simple and accessible resource with an easy learning curve, which will help ensure your success.

Three main dollhouse miniature scales are used and you can apply them instantly to your miniature gardens: 1-inch scale, also known as large size, ½-inch scale or medium size, and ¼-inch scale or small size. Each unit—1 inch, ½ inch, or ¼ inch—is equal to 1 foot in full size. Let's walk through these scales so you can start sizing up your miniature garden space and get started.

LEFT: *One-inch scale, or large size, is chosen for this container, since it's wider than 10 inches.*

RIGHT: *A specific focal point usually dictates the scale of a garden.*

LEFT: *This chaise lounge is 2½ inches tall, which is 1-inch scale or large size.*

RIGHT: *This Easter Island replica, surrounded by 'Roly-Poly' hens and chicks, is medium size, or ½-inch scale.*

**LARGE SIZE MINIATURES** In the large size, or 1-inch scale, 1 inch is equal to 1 foot. In this scale, a 6-foot-tall man would become 6 inches tall. There is a direct and simple correlation of the number of full-sized feet to large miniature size inches; a 5-foot shovel will be 5 inches, a 1-foot-wide pot is 1 inch wide, and a 40-foot-long garden bed is 40 inches long. This scale is popular in bigger miniature gardens because it is easy calculate, easy to handle, and you can see the accessories at a distance. Choose this scale for inground gardens and for pots larger than 10 inches wide. Using too-large accessories in a too-small pot will look crowded. Conversely, tiny accessories in a large pot look like they're swimming. You might think to just add more accessories to fill up the scene, but then the miniature garden can look cluttered.

**MEDIUM SIZE MINIATURES** In medium size, a ½-inch miniature is equal to 1 foot in full size; a 6-foot-tall man in ½-inch scale will be 3 inches tall, a 5-foot shovel will be 2½ inches long, a 1-foot-wide pot will be ½ inch wide, and a 40-foot garden bed will be 20 inches long. This size fits well in pots 5 to 10 inches wide and is ideal for centerpieces and tablescapes.

*A fairy garden in small size, or ¼-inch scale.*

**SMALL SIZE MINIATURES** In the small size, ¼ inch is equal to 1 foot in full size. A 6-foot-tall man in the ¼-inch scale is 1½ inches tall, a 5-foot shovel will be 1¼ inches long, the 1-foot-wide pot is now ¼ inch wide, and your 40-foot garden bed is 10 inches long. You can see how diminutive this scale can be, but it is delightful in tiny pots, or for making a miniature garden in a terrarium. Containers that are 2 to 5 inches can make sweet vignettes for the windowsill. Or bring a tiny garden to your next dinner party as a hostess gift, and you'll have a friend for life.

## THE NEW MATH

Take a minute to digest this new math and you can start to see the sense in it. The ½-inch scale is half of the 1-inch scale, and the ¼-inch scale is half of the ½-inch scale. It sounds confusing at first, but it will get easier with a bit of practice.

Now, there is no law saying that you have to use this scale with that garden, but once again, I'll emphasize the importance of considering where your miniature garden will live and how it will be viewed. For example, larger pots tend to be placed closer to the ground, or to sit right on the ground, so the garden is, at most times, a few feet away from our perspective as adults. By using the large size inground, you are able to see your miniature garden from farther away, from your kitchen window or your back deck. Using bigger accessories, and bigger plants, will help your miniature garden be appreciated and seen.

*Small size accessories add interest to a row of tiny pots.*

# BIG FUN WITH TINY SPACES

*Within the miniature garden world, there's still small, medium, and large. This 1-inch scale chair is considered large size.*

Miniature garden accessories are as plentiful as places to grow miniature gardens, and are available in many sizes—so how do you choose which style and size to use? Select accessories that are too big for a small tablescape, or a tiny chair that doesn't fit on the patio, and the realism is lost. Enchantment happens when everything is in proper scale.

Larger scales are ideal for inground gardens because you can see them from a standing position, by walking past, or when sitting several feet away. You don't want your efforts to go unnoticed or unappreciated, so select 1-inch scale accessories, or large size. We also rely on 1-inch scale accessories for pots that are 10 inches wide or more, simply because it would take too many medium (½-inch scale) or small (¼-inch scale) accessories to create a presence.

For miniature gardens that are 10 inches wide or less, medium size or ½-inch accessories are perfect. They are small enough that you can fit a patio set of chairs and a table onto a 4-inch round patio quite comfortably. Use the ¼-inch scale for 2-inch gardens or tiny terrariums.

An advantage of working in miniature is that your choices do not have to be permanent. You can completely change the personality of your scene quickly and easily by just swapping out accessories, or by replacing plants seasonally or yearly. Creating a miniature garden is a far cry from planting a magnolia tree in the corner of your backyard and leaving it there forever. The plants we use for miniature gardening can be moved or repotted in minutes.

## THE SIZE OF PLANTS

When it comes to scale and size, plants offer more flexibility than other items in a miniature garden. This is because the miniature or dwarf trees and shrubs you will use can be pushed to fit different scales. A six-inch-tall tree can be appropriate for different scales—it can translate to a six-foot-tall tree in large size, or a twelve-foot-tall tree in medium size. If there is no bench, birdbath, or patio beside the tree, the miniature scale will not register, and the tree is just a plant in a pot.

A popular example is the trough garden. This type of garden is usually planted in hypertufa pots with miniature and dwarf conifers nestled in with mosses and low-growing groundcovers. Trough gardens are beautiful in and of themselves, but if you place a miniature birdbath in the trough, you instantly have a scaled reference that you can see and use to measure in your head how small the garden is. Remove the miniature birdbath and there is no accessory to relate to—the container becomes a simple trough garden again.

*The trunk of this healthy, growing tree is about one inch thick.*

# SHRINKING THE DESIGN RULES

Let's say you've explored your indoor and outdoor spaces, and deliberated a bit. You have chosen the spot where you want your miniature garden to live. You've decided upon the scale, and you are ready to think about your design.

We now turn to full-sized garden rules to lay the groundwork. Using the basic garden tenets of anchor point, balance, layers, texture, color, and focal point, you can plan your miniature garden with confidence. Understanding all of these elements will help you design like a professional and create a lasting, enchanting miniature garden.

Any design process is mixed with a variety of elements; creating a garden is no different in complexity than designing a dress or the interior of a room. You need to know what to look for first, and how the pieces come together into one design. For example, when identifying the anchor point of the garden, you need to consider the balance, too; as you layer plants, textures need to be considered. This may seem complicated, but it is part of the creative fun of designing a garden. More important for the gardening beginner, it will reduce the sometimes overwhelming range of options to a very manageable number, allowing you to get started right away.

LEFT: *This hen and chick is perfect for a small terracotta pot.*

RIGHT: *Several focal points in this houseboat scene keep the viewer motivated to look closer.*

ABOVE: *Miniature garden design follows the rules of full-sized gardening, but everything is viewed in one eyeful.*

BELOW: *A one-foot-tall 'Compressa' juniper translates to a believable tree next to a small footbridge.*

LEFT: *Well-shaped trees, like this 'Pixie Dust' dwarf Alberta spruce, make excellent anchor points.*

RIGHT: *Layering plants and accessories gives your garden realism and depth.*

**ANCHOR POINTS** An anchor point in a full-sized garden is usually the largest element: perhaps a planting that is already there and cannot be easily moved. It could be a tall tree in the corner of your yard or, a big fountain that has been there forever, or your deck off the kitchen in the back of the house. Anchor points are also called jumping-off points by designers of full-sized gardens, because the anchors must be part of the design; there is no choice but to work with them. However, in the miniature garden world, an anchor point could be just about anything because you are creating your own scene from scratch. To capture authenticity and realism, use a miniature version of any full-sized anchor point. This can be as simple as the tallest (or only) tree.

**LAYERS** Layering is a design technique you might not think to consider for such a small garden, but it is actually critical to a beautiful scene. Just as in your full-sized garden, layering creates dimensionality and visual interest. Once you have established your anchor point, you can start layering with different plant heights, creating the boundaries or walls of your garden and helping the plants' transitions between each other. For example, an eight-inch-tall dwarf hinoki cypress and two-inch-tall dwarf mondo grass, planted with half-inch-tall 'Elfin' thyme, creates three layers in a miniature garden bed.

LEFT: *Everything in a miniature gardens is seen all at once, so balance is essential.*

RIGHT: *Playing with form, the globe-shaped canopy of this 'Elf' dwarf Alberta spruce mimics the shape of its container.*

**BALANCE** Miniature garden design is much more condensed than full-sized garden planning because the tiny scene is usually viewed all at once, in one eyeful. In a standard-sized garden, one corner of the garden, or one garden bed, is viewed at a time, so there needs to be balance within that section and with the rest of the garden. When you consider balance in the miniature garden, you are judging the complete view of everything all at once: the size of the pot or inground space, shape of the garden bed, tree height and form, size of the patio, and anything else you want to include. It all has to have a pleasing equilibrium, so no one thing overwhelms and distracts from the others. Let your instincts guide you, and as you start to pull the pieces together, be sure to stand back and look at the garden as a whole— getting a glimpse of the finished product.

**FORM** Form is important because you don't want all the plants in your miniature garden to be the same shape. Miniature and dwarf plants and trees come in as many forms as full-sized plants. Upright narrow, broad, spreading, globular, and trailing are just some of the overall plant shapes. Combine tall, narrow trees with globe-shaped shrubs, include a trailing groundcover, and you've combined a trio of interesting forms that are layered nicely, will be balanced in shape, and are great for any medium-sized pot.

LEFT: *Don't be afraid of bold color in your miniature garden.*

RIGHT: *Include contrasting textures and colors for added interest.*

**TEXTURE** Texture in garden design refers to variety in foliage. A small boxwood tree with tiny, broad leaves has a completely different texture than a spiky-needled mugo pine. The small but thick leaves of a groundcover sedum have a chunky texture, compared to those of finely textured woolly thyme. Combine contrasting textures to create a more interesting design and define the plants in your garden bed.

**COLOR** Color is an exciting component of miniature design that is often overlooked by the fledgling gardener. Stop to notice on your next trip to the local nursery, and you'll find that there are a variety of greens, from light and bright to dark and rich. Blue-greens can vary from almost gray to a bluish turquoise. To create a vibrant design, keep one primary foliage color consistent throughout the garden. Too many variations of the same color in such a small garden can look aimless and unplanned. Add interest with contrasting foliage, miniature brown sedge, or one of the chocolate-colored sedums, for example.

**FOCAL POINTS** The focal point in a garden is the element the eye is most drawn to. What is the difference between an anchor point and a focal point? The anchor point is usually the largest natural element—often the tallest tree. In both full-sized and miniature gardens, the focal point is often a functional or décor component: a fountain, garden sculpture, or bench at the end of a path. One of the secrets to miniature gardening is that the focal point sets the scale, with other garden elements relating to that feature. Once a tiny bench is added, the plants that surround it suddenly shift in your mind's eye to the scale of the bench.

Because you are creating your garden from scratch, and ideally have no focal point already established, you have the luxury of creating your own. Birdbaths and seating areas are popular eye-catchers, but if you have something special—perhaps a memento from a cherished trip—by all means, make it your focal point.

*The more interesting the focal point, the more intriguing the garden.*

# NOW GO FORTH

You can take all of these miniature design rules, follow them to a "T", and create a spectacular garden. Or, you can use none of them, see where your heart's desire leads you—and still create a spectacular garden. But if you do find something lacking in your miniature garden and can't quite identify what it is, come back to these design rules and see if an element is missing. Keep in mind that even the most experienced gardeners move and add things when creating a new garden. That's part of the fun of doing things in miniature—instead of spending hours changing out plants in a full-sized garden, you can spend minutes renovating your tiny plot.

This unique blend of craft and gardening isn't just about design and creation. The act of growing your miniature garden makes up a good part of the hobby. Watching your miniature plants weave together through the months and years, and seeing your miniature tree—the one you planted years ago—grow a nice thick trunk and branches is wonderfully rewarding. If you're excited about that pint-sized masterpiece you just planted, wait until it grows up. My bet is that by then, you'll be thoroughly hooked on the world of miniature gardening.

*Everyone loves a small garden that tells a story.*

## WALKING THE
## MINIATURE TALK
### PATIOS AND PATHWAYS

TO ENSURE THE REALISM that creates
enchantment, these critical elements are
necessary: plants, accessories, and a patio
or pathway. The planned, intentional aspect
of a patio or walkway immediately signals to
the viewer that this is no ordinary planting
in a pot, teasing them to come in for a closer
view. Hardscapes also convey the scale of
the garden, and lend an important contrast
to plantings, providing a pleasing richness.

*Tiny blossoms and a diminutive
figure rim a flagstone patio.*

Paths can be especially alluring. Just a hint of a walkway triggers curiosity—just a few stones or miniature pavers can do the trick. A surprise at the path's end rewards the viewer: a quiet bench beside a birdbath, a chair next to a tiny stump table, or a pond made with a piece of tumbled blue glass and a wee frog.

Knowing the choices for patio materials, where to find them, and how they should be installed helps ensure success.

## BUILDING BLOCKS OF A MINIATURE HARDSCAPE

The materials you use for your miniature patio or path can make or break the garden's realism and theme. Using chunky, brightly colored marbles as a pathway through the garden bed would be like paving your garden path in bowling balls. If it isn't done in real life, it won't look realistic in miniature, either. Another example is a formal miniature garden with perfect symmetry, adorned with marble-like Romanesque pedestals, flanked by 'Sky Pencil' Japanese holly on both sides—with a craggy flagstone patio. Combining rustic rock with such formal accessories and trees would clash in the mind's eye, spoiling the effect.

Different materials aid different themes, and by using authentic patio materials you can ensure perfect replication and the instant recognition you're hoping for. Almost any medium used in full-sized gardens is available in miniature, or can be broken down into smaller pieces. Tiny pebbles can look like gravel, miniature brick can be weathered and stained to look old, and small, ⅜-inch river rocks can make a very realistic cobblestone path. Ultimately, it is your private world, so go ahead and use bright yellow crushed glass or pennies as pavers. But if you are after realism, opt for authentic patio materials.

Borders are a key factor in creating your garden and keeping it tamed; they will draw the line—literally and figuratively—between patios and paths and plant beds. The faux wood border edging featured in many miniature gardens is a thin, flexible plastic that bends easily. You can create a specific shape, or staple it into a circle and hold it in place with a couple of skewers. Plastic borders can also be folded and creased to make a sharp corner, for a geometric look. You can find real wood borders, too, at your local woodworking or hardware store. Real wood will age gracefully and last a couple of seasons before it begins to rot.

*Mini patio mix anchors irregular flagstones.*

## SIZING WHAT'S UNDERFOOT

The size or scale of your garden will dictate the size of patio materials you use. Envision the patio that you want to create in human size first. You can estimate size easily by relating it to your own foot, because miniature scaling uses foot-length measurements as part of the ratio. Picture stepping on the bricks, stone, or gravel with your own feet and you can get an idea of the approximate size without needing a ruler. A brick averages eight inches long. Compare that to a nine-inch-long foot (average), scale it down to one-inch scale, and you can see that a miniature brick should be a little over a half inch long.

The theme of the garden will tell you how big the patio should be in proportion to the garden bed. If you are making a backyard scene, complete with a picnic table and miniature barbecue, you will need a bigger patio on which to place these items, because at full size, we would allow plenty of room to navigate around the grill and the table. A little reading nook vignette with a chair and a flowerpot requires a much smaller patio to make the scene look inviting and cozy.

*Pleurocarpous moss fills the spaces on this rock walkway.*

LEFT: *A tiny pathway leads the eye through the scene and creates a story.*

RIGHT: *Can't decide between a patio and a path? Include both.*

If you are just starting out, you may want to use the rule of thirds to estimate patio size. That is, the garden bed should make up two-thirds of the area, and the patio should take up the last third. A twelve-inch-diameter pot, for example, would look nicely balanced with a patio area of about four inches by four inches. Or, if your theme demands a larger patio area, make the garden bed one-third of the overall size of the pot, and give two-thirds to the patio. You can always adjust this area as you are building your miniature garden and go with what looks best, but it's a good way to estimate the amount of materials you will need.

Marble, tile, rocks, flagstone, and pebbles are full-sized materials that can be miniaturized and are readily available. High-fired miniature bricks mounted on sheets of mesh have the ability to last for years. Tumbled glass adds yet another dimension.

Other potential materials include super-fine sand (available at miniature garden stores). This sand is a perfect scale for miniature beaches, as regular play sand tends to be a bit chunky for the miniature perfectionist. Bark mulch sifted down to crumbs makes a very believable playground area; create a path with the crumbs and line it with miniature logs to replicate a park trail.

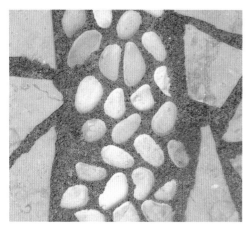

**MARBLE AND CERAMIC TILE** Using marble as a material in your garden will add instant formality. Its rich colors translate well in even the smallest gardens. Ceramic tile is a bit more casual in appearance; some tiles available today can take on the look of flagstone, which add authenticity. Color-match your patio material to your pot, or the garden's decor, to crank up the charm factor dramatically. Neutral colors will make the patio blend into the garden; brighter colors will make it pop.

Marble and tile are often found in one-foot-square units. Your garage is the first place to look, though—remember those leftovers from the kitchen or bathroom remodel? If you don't have remnants, ask a friend, neighbor, or family member. Chances are, someone you know has a piece or two they'd be happy to donate to your effort. If you're coming up short, try recycled building material centers, thrift stores, or local tile stores. Even if you have to buy a small piece, it's usually not too costly.

LEFT: *Mix materials for added interest.*

RIGHT: *Blue spruce seedlings anchor this eclectic garden.*

LEFT: *Try a marble perimeter with a matching flagstone path down the center.*

RIGHT: *Three different hardscapes set off a 'Jervis' Canada hemlock.*

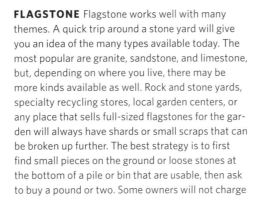

**FLAGSTONE** Flagstone works well with many themes. A quick trip around a stone yard will give you an idea of the many types available today. The most popular are granite, sandstone, and limestone, but, depending on where you live, there may be more kinds available as well. Rock and stone yards, specialty recycling stores, local garden centers, or any place that sells full-sized flagstones for the garden will always have shards or small scraps that can be broken up further. The best strategy is to first find small pieces on the ground or loose stones at the bottom of a pile or bin that are usable, then ask to buy a pound or two. Some owners will not charge you, but even if they do, it should only cost a few dollars.

Most of the rocks will be irregular, so choose the flattest side of the stone for the top of the patio. Either press the stone lightly into the soil, or dig a little soil out of the spot and place the rock, gently pushing the soil to fill in the empty space underneath. Work methodically from one side to the other, keeping the space between stones consistent across the patio. Sweep soil between all the spaces after you've finished laying the tile, then use a water sprayer to mist the entire area, to settle the soil and wash off the stones.

**MINIATURE BRICKS** Miniature bricks are just perfect for tiny gardens. Mounted on a mesh sheet, the bricks' warm terracotta color and well-known pattern instantly relate familiarity and scale to any viewer. The brick sheets are high-fired, strong, and last much longer outdoors than low-fired single bricks. Extended freezing will crack and break terracotta bricks, but short, intermittent freezes are not as damaging, it seems.

Stores specializing in miniatures carry a number of different brick sheets. Ask for real terracotta bricks. Because they are genuine terracotta, though, they will weather differently in different gardens. Note that loose miniature bricks are low-fired and will not survive overhead watering for more than a few months. Loose bricks are best used inside, where you can water the plants gently from the back of the container. You can also find mixes of faux used brick to simulate a worn and weathered look.

Sheets of real terracotta bricks are only available in one-inch scale and can be cut with heavy-duty kitchen scissors. You can create a sleek look by arranging pieces in different patterns, cutting the sheet to fit into a curvy space, and trimming the patio in a brick border—or you can add complexity to your design with different pebbles or flagstone.

LEFT: *A mix of faux used brick lends detail and interest.*

RIGHT: *Have fun with the color of the patio and coordinate it with containers, plantings, and accessories.*

## Breaking up is (not) hard to do

Turning too-large marble, ceramic tile, or flagstone pieces into usable fragments can be fun and therapeutic—and a bit dangerous or damaging to your surroundings. When any of these materials are broken apart with a chisel or sledgehammer, the shards can fly and nick or ding anything they hit, including people, cars, and pets. A fast and inexpensive way to corral the pieces is to use a big cardboard box, opened and placed on its side. Do the messy work in front of the box, using the flaps to help direct the flying shards into the box, instead of the shining exterior of your spouse's freshly waxed car.

A concrete garage floor is usually the handiest surface on which to break apart stone, for a couple of reasons. First, you need a hard surface to work on; brick, stone, a concrete basement floor, or the corner of a driveway or sidewalk would also work. Softer surfaces, like a wooden potting bench, for example, will be too bouncy. You'll fight the material and it won't break apart easily. The second reason for working on the floor is that you can get on top of the tile and gravity helps the momentum of the sledgehammer on the chisel. If this sounds too difficult, there are a variety of new chisels out there that have a protective shield on the handle to save you from whacking your other hand with the hammer. This type of chisel is strongly recommended for anyone who does not have a lot of experience with hammers.

Use a face shield, then get down on one knee and hold the piece of tile with your toe. With a chisel and hammer, break apart the sheet by chiseling away the straight edges of the tile. You never see a straight edge in full-sized patio stones, so get rid of those right away. Then you can focus on what you have.

One swift swing of the hammer should make a break close to where you want. Marble tile tends to break wherever it wants, but it sometimes helps to use the corner of the chisel. Some marble will not break easily; in this case, use the corner of the sledgehammer.

Using the chisel minimizes the damage done to the surface of the material, whereas the edge or corner of a sledgehammer head will make a bigger mark. That mark may stand out, but it does fade over time. Most ceramic tile chisels apart like butter.

The trick to having marble and tile pieces look like real patio materials is to make them all relatively the same size. You may not be able to break them exactly at the spot you want, but you can make the sizes similar. Pieces that are about one and a half inches square are ideal for one-inch scale; make them less than one inch for half-inch scale. The littlest pieces can be used for quarter-inch scale gardens or terrarium vignettes.

*A secluded patio hideaway*
*adds mystery to your garden.*

**STONE AND MOSAIC SHEETS** Stone sheets are rocks that, like bricks, are glued onto a mesh sheet so you can lay the whole sheet at once. Meant as accents for full-sized baths and kitchens, stone sheets can easily be adapted for the miniature garden. They're easy to cut and install, and provide the desired rock patio look without the tedious work. A variety of great color schemes and textures are now available at larger hardware centers or miniature garden stores.

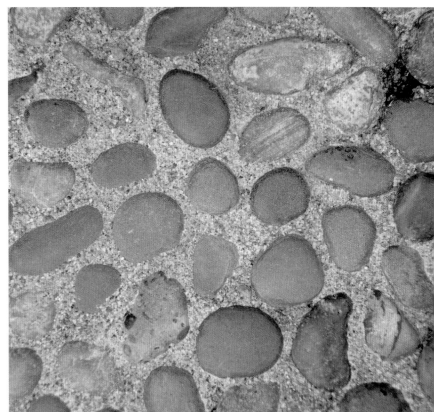

LEFT: *Smooth miniature rocks come in sheets that allow for easy cutting and sizing.*

RIGHT: *A patio of smooth, rounded-edge stones awaits accessories—or not.*

**GLASS** Tumbled glass adds depth to a patio, which is something you wouldn't normally see in full-sized gardens, but the availability of colors make it a fun choice for fantasy-themed scenes. An added benefit of glass is that it will never fade in the sun and is a great alternative for hotter climates. Note that it's tumbled, not broken, glass that you want. The edges of broken glass pieces are extremely sharp; tumbling smoothes them down so you can handle them safely. You might remember to watch for sharp edges on your miniature patio, but your neighbor's toddler might not.

Recycling stores, glass studios, craft stores, and some garden centers will have tumbled glass for sale, in many colors. Florists often use it in vases. Look for pieces with one flat side and use that for the patio's surface. Make sure pieces are flush and level with one another.

As much as miniature gardens can be slaves to realism, remember that you can still have fun, especially with patios. The secret is making sure features that aren't true-to-life still match the overall theme. Want color? Pick a theme like a circus or birthday party. Love one particular color? Use the patio to bring that favorite hue into the scene.

ABOVE: *Part patio, part path, this blue glass divider separates planting areas.*

BELOW: *Opaque green glass creates a striking miniature hardscape.*

**MINIATURE PEBBLES** Tiny pebbles can easily look like gravel in the miniature garden. Larger pebbles can look like cobblestones. You can find miniature pebbles in pet stores, garden centers, florists, craft stores, online, at the beach, or you could bring some home from a special vacation. Model railroad stores carry ballast, a miniature gray gravel used to level railroad tracks. The size of the pebbles should reflect the size of the garden; it is handy to have your garden scale already decided.

A smart trick is to cover the area where you'll be placing the miniature pebbles with a landscape cloth or screen-door mesh cut to size. This will prevent your small pebbles from getting mixed up in the soil and make it easier to redo the garden when the time comes, as the pebbles will be clean and free of soil.

Choose pebbles to suit your theme. Smooth, rounded stones in pinks, creams, and browns help to create a peaceful scene. A bright blue cobalt patio, with white and red accents, makes a perfect Fourth of July garden. Speckled black and white crushed granite lends formality, just as it does in full-sized garden design.

*Pebbles in green and brown shades complement engraved decorative stones.*

## LOCK 'EM IN

You can create permanent patios with a specialized, dry cement-based mix specifically designed for miniature patios, usually called mini patio mix. The mix is layered in while dry, so you have time to piece together your patio before misting it down and activating the cement. Regular concrete is too bulky, and standard outdoor grout is not as realistic because it's too smooth. More important, both concrete and grout need to be wet for handling—a significant drawback for our purposes. You would have to poke pieces into the wet mixture, and the patio surface would end up uneven. Using a dry mini patio mix, you can take your time and make a pleasing design. When brick or stone sheets are locked in with this specialized patio mix, they can last for years and won't wash away in the rain during watering.

I recommend planting your garden bed before you lay the patio. Most dry patio mixes require several days of curing before planting beds around them, so by doing the beds before the patio, you can build the garden all in one afternoon and have a complete miniature garden to enjoy while the path cures.

## YOUR PATIO OVER TIME

Whatever your miniature patio is made of, it will age. Go with it. Let the moss find its way into the cracks, let the garden bed spill over the border—it just adds to the authenticity and realism. Or, not. You can always use a paintbrush as a broom and manicure scissors as clippers and spend a quiet moment coaxing your garden back into shape.

LEFT: *Patios and stone features can be kept tidy, or allowed to age naturally with the surrounding garden.*

RIGHT: *Mini patio mix locks in stones for a lasting hardscape.*

# IT'S A SMALL WORLD
## PLANTS FOR THE MINIATURE GARDEN

WHEN YOU START searching for plants to use in your miniature garden, you will discover an entirely new world of growing things. The experienced full-sized gardener may benefit from seeing plants on a smaller scale. New gardeners will appreciate the scope and range of tiny plant options.

*All this cozy scene needs is a tall glass of iced tea and you.*

As with standard-sized gardening, your plant preferences will change with your skill level and tastes as you learn more about the hobby. Growth rate, leaf size, and ease of care are all important factors to consider, but nothing is carved in stone. For example, a tree that is labeled to grow at least three inches per year may grow less than one inch per year on your back deck. You'll find the same number of variables in miniature gardening as in full-sized gardening, which makes this hobby an ever-evolving pursuit.

## WHAT TO LOOK FOR

As a plant description, the term "miniature" refers to the growth rate rather than the size of the plant. Miniature is defined as growing less than one inch per year, with a minimum height after ten years of six to ten inches and a maximum height and width of less than three feet after many years.

When plants and containers are chosen with scale and growth rate in mind, a miniature garden can last for years before the plants become rootbound and in need of repotting. Inground, once plants get established during the first year, the garden becomes low maintenance and will need only

a few minutes of care a week—versus the regular hours it takes to maintain a full-sized garden. Slow-growing plants will extend the life of your miniature garden, keeping it small and allowing the plants to weave together over time. Once the miniature garden has aged and weathered, it often achieves the authenticity and charm you're looking for.

Foliage size is a critical factor in choosing miniature garden plants. For example, young ficus trees usually have a wonderful little trunk and a great branching habit, but the leaves can look too big in miniature scenes unless the accompanying plants and accessories are matched in correct scale. Trunk size, stems, leaves, needles, and branches must all be in the right proportion to each other. Just because it is a small plant does not make it a realistic miniature plant. Look for varieties that truly mimic full-sized plants.

Ease of care is also a consideration for most people. If a garden is overplanted with fast-growing plants, things can quickly go wrong when growing speeds up in the summer. Not paying attention to watering for as little as a day or two can lead to a dried-up miniature garden that cannot be revived—all because it was overplanted to begin with. By taking the maintenance of the plants into consideration from the start, you can avoid disappointment later.

ABOVE: *A variety of dwarf plants adorn this stone path.*

BELOW LEFT: *The diminutive bloom of tree of a thousand stars (*Serissa foetida*) seems to reflect the bloom pattern carved in the stone at its base.*

BELOW RIGHT: *Rows of colors and textures, waiting for the right miniature garden.*

*'Cis' dwarf Korean fir* (Abies
koreana *'Cis'*) *is a popular choice
for small container settings.*

*Around paths and patios, small hens and chicks provide an interesting border.*

# TRUE MINIATURE TREES

Miniature forms of regular trees and shrubs generally have the plant's characteristic foliage, just on a smaller or shorter scale. These true miniatures are naturally stunted regular trees that are propagated for their smaller leaf size and slower growth rates. They are called mutants, sports, or witch's brooms, depending on where the new or distorted growth is found on the mother plant. A miniature tree will still grow up; it just takes a long time to do so. This slowness is precisely what we can take advantage of.

For example, the 150-foot-tall Alberta spruce found in forests has a miniature version—'Jean's Dilly' dwarf spruce (*Picea glauca* 'Jean's Dilly'). It takes about twenty years to reach six feet. Trees that mimic a large, full-sized version are ideal for gardening in miniature. Because they are the same trees we see growing in our landscapes, we can easily relate to them at any scale.

Another example of a standard tree that has a miniature version is the hinoki cypress (*Chamaecyparis obtusa*). Some full-sized versions have an ultimate height of sixty-five feet by sixteen feet wide, growing at a rate of approximately one foot per year. In comparison, the true miniature varieties grow a half inch per year, with an ultimate height of two feet—forty-eight years to reach twenty-four inches! You can take advantage of that slow growth rate for years in a miniature garden.

LEFT: *The 'Ellie B.' hinoki cypress* (Chamaecyparis obtusa *'Ellie B.') is a true miniature.*

RIGHT: *Always note a plant's growth rate to make sure it is truly a miniature garden staple.*

## DWARF TREES AND SHRUBS

LEFT: *Needles on this 'Jamy' balsam fir are a delicate copy of those on larger conifers.*

RIGHT: *Check tags for key information on growth rate and planting needs.*

The term "dwarf" is used very casually in the horticultural world, and is often misunderstood as a plant description. Dwarf indicates a growth rate of one to six inches per year. Six inches per year is monumental when you are working in miniature, and dwarf trees that grow that fast will soon be too large for a miniature garden. Look for dwarf trees and shrubs that grow no more than two or three inches per year.

Plant retailers have discovered that cute sells. A plant is sometimes named for marketing purposes—dwarf translates to small, small translates to cute. But the name is not always horticulturally correct. Always note the botanical name, and look for the growth rate on the tag or in the plant information. This is why gardeners often rely on botanical rather than common names for plants—it's easy to be misled if a grower wants to sell plants fast.

# BONSAI TREES

Bonsai is a form of miniature gardening that originated in China centuries ago—more proof that the miniature hobby is far from a new trend. New miniature gardeners often think of planting bonsai trees in their tiny plots, but it's important to note that growing bonsai and miniature gardening are different activities.

Bonsai trees have been trained to grow small by having their roots trimmed to fit into a shallow pot. The restricted roots send a message to the plant to stay small in order to survive. Because of the limited nourishment received through the roots and soil, bonsais must be fed and tended constantly. When a bonsai is repotted into a regular pot for a miniature garden, it may look great for a short time but the tree can die from having too much root space all at once. The water will not be confined like it was in the bonsai dish, will wick away into the soil, and will not get absorbed by the roots.

Remember also that it is the confined root system that tells the plant to stay small. When the bonsai is suddenly planted in deeper, more luxurious soil, it may grow into the full-sized plant it really is.

How do you know if a particular plant will work in a miniature setting? I have heard many stories of miniature gardens not lasting a season because what the gardener thought was a miniature tree, was not. It looked good, and fit immediately into the garden scene, but then outgrew the pot in less than one season. Bonsai and plants with miniature or dwarf designation are the kinds of plants that can be used with a degree of certainty.

*Dwarf plants can be cared for and trained to create a bonsai effect.*

## *Workaround for using bonsai*

If you really want to use bonsai in your miniature garden, plant the whole pot right into the miniature garden container, pot and all. Bury the bonsai's pot up to the same ground level of the original bonsai and leave the nebari (the visible surface roots growing at the lower trunk of the tree) exposed for more interest. Monitor the bonsai very carefully for the first few weeks to figure out the correct amount of water; it may need less because it is a pot inside of a pot. Look often for signs of stress. Browning leaves or needles might mean too much water; withered leaves may signal not enough.

You will need to dig up the bonsai periodically to root-prune it, the same way you do regular bonsai. Note that you will need to top-prune, wire, and maintain your tree following bonsai instructions, too. The only thing that may change is the water schedule. As with full-sized gardening, the best way to read the moisture content of your bonsai is to stick your finger into the soil and follow the instructions for that plant.

*This bonsai is planted, pot and all, into a larger container as part of a miniature scene.*

## HEY BABY!

Floral sections in home and garden centers often sell young (not specifically miniature) plants in two- or four-inch pots that are temptingly cute and small. These may or may not come with a plant tag that shows the name and growth rate. A baby plant can work, if you know what it is and how fast it grows and can adjust accordingly. Just realize that you may be replanting your miniature garden within the season, or the year, because these so-called babies can become full-sized quite quickly.

## HERBS ARE HERBS

Herb starts are a good example of mistaking young plants for miniature plants. These colorful, richly textured, often lovely smelling options, in little four-inch pots, are tempting—but don't be fooled. A young sage plant can look like a sweet little banana palm tree, but it will want to grow to at least twelve inches tall by twelve inches wide in the first season. A wee rosemary plant can resemble a miniature shrub—but its natural size is four feet by four feet. Baby herbs will more than quadruple in size before you are halfway through the summer, so save them for large, inground, Barbie-sized gardens or fairy scenes, where they will have room to grow and be what they are meant to be.

LEFT: *New growth on this tiny 'Loowit' Japanese hemlock provides a pleasing contrast to darker old growth.*

RIGHT: *Red thyme is perfect atop this miniature stone edifice.*

## TYPES OF PLANTS

With trees and shrubs in general—full-sized and miniature—there are different types of foliage to consider: broadleaf evergreen, broadleaf deciduous, and conifers. Whether you like needles, evergreen foliage, or colorful autumn leaves, careful choices can make a miniature theme sing.

This overview covers most of the available types of trees and shrubs for outdoor miniature gardens.

LEFT: *They may be small, but these purple blooms pack a visual punch.*

RIGHT: *This inground bed offers a bit of room to roam.*

LEFT: *Evergreen foliage ensures a secluded spot to rock year-round.*

CENTER: *This spirea has light, airy foliage and clusters of feathery pink blooms.*

RIGHT: *Tiny white blossoms of 'Majestic' Japanese holly are striking against its evergreen leaves.*

**BROADLEAF EVERGREEN** Broadleaf plants have wide leaves, as opposed to needles like a pine tree. Evergreen means they keep their leaves in the fall, and they stay green throughout the year. This kind of plant is great for adding texture to your garden. Mix broadleaf evergreens with conifers and either match or complement other plant colors for a professionally designed look.

**DECIDUOUS BROADLEAF** Deciduous plants lose their leaves in the fall before going dormant in the winter. Most deciduous plants used in full-sized gardening are broadleaf. By identifying a plant by the term "deciduous broadleaf," you answer several questions at once as to its behavior and look.

In a miniature garden, witnessing the change in seasons is quite magical. Deciduous trees and shrubs can enhance the seasonal experience, especially if other companion plants stay green. When choosing plants, try to match or complement the trunk and stem colors of your deciduous plants with the colors of the evergreens.

## TRUE MINIATURE AND DWARF CONIFERS

Conifers are trees that bear cones. They are the largest family of trees in the world, including the tallest and smallest trees. They are hardy, adaptable, colorful, and grow in many patterns and forms. Thankfully, horticulturists have discovered the beauty of miniature conifers in recent years; they are perfect for small gardens because they truly look like a full-sized tree in miniature.

A conifer in your miniature garden can provide the look of a majestic tree on a tiny scale, especially when it is left to grow for a period of time. You can easily mimic life-sized landscapes in miniature with the many choices of conifers available today. As mentioned, however, be wary. There is a difference between true slow-growing conifers and baby conifers. A baby blue spruce may take years to grow from seed, but once the tree begins to mature, the growth rate increases dramatically. It is the consistently slow-growing conifers that are successful in miniature garden settings, and with the variety available today, there should be multiple choices for every climate.

Conifers offer a variety of miniature options and are preferred for a number of reasons. They are easy to grow when placed in the right spot with the right soil and light. There are choices for a range of climates. They are excellently priced for the beginning gardener, especially if you start with a young conifer in a four-inch pot. Whether you are mimicking a backyard scene with an anchor point, or creating a wee forest, you'll almost always get the results you want from the conifer family.

LEFT: *Whatever color or texture you're hoping to find, chances are there's a miniature conifer to fit the bill.*

RIGHT: *A blend of evergreen and deciduous plants give this sitting area a lush richness.*

LEFT: *In the springtime, conifers burst with fresh, colorful buds like this dwarf Canada hemlock.*

RIGHT: *In winter, conifers can turn vivid colors. This is known as winter blush.*

**TRY A TREE** Miniature gardening newbies are sometimes intimidated by growing a small living tree and opt to stick to groundcovers. Don't be scared away from trees. A garden with only low-growing groundcovers lacks the sense of permanence a tree can bring to the setting. As in full-sized gardens, the trees and shrubs you plant are the bones of the garden. Everything else changes: the bedding plants, annuals, groundcovers, and perennials that make up the understory of the garden all eventually need dividing, reseed, regrow, and get moved or replanted. But trees and shrubs are the lasting backdrop for your garden design. These anchors allow you play with seasonal plants and accessories as often as you like.

Another reward for planting a miniature tree is that in only a couple of years you will have a miniature tree with a big-tree look: a thicker trunk, tree-like branches, and a grand canopy. Young conifers are appealing in four-inch pots at the nursery, and they are great candidates for miniature gardens, but they're much more interesting when they start acquiring an aged look; in fact, it's the same look the bonsai masters strive for, but with a fraction of the work.

Even little trees can have a majestic look—just prune the bottom-most branches to expose more trunk. When a conifer outgrows its spot in one miniature garden pot or bed, just use it to start another, larger inground miniature garden, or used it in a new container scene.

LEFT: Bellium minutum *in bloom is a sea of tiny daisies.*

RIGHT: *'Platt's Black' brass buttons is a contrast of colors.*

**MINIATURE GARDEN BEDDING PLANTS** In full-sized gardens, there are several layers of greenery, all of which help direct the eye where you would like it to go. For example, the top layer is often a tall tree, the middle layer a medium-height shrub, and the bedding plants make up the layer closest to the ground. We look to bedding plants to add interest and complement the trees and shrubs.

Groundcovers, rockery plants, mini succulents, perennials, and low-growing, small-leaved creepers can all be miniatures, but they are very different plants. The categories are plants that grow small and plants that can be kept small. One of the advantages of gardening in miniature is the low maintenance. Plants that grow slow and small, as opposed to ones that are kept small, are a lot easier to manage. 'Elfin' thyme is a favorite low-maintenance groundcover because it's well behaved, with tiny leaves that form a thick mat and spread slowly along the ground. On the other hand, if your miniature bed is the only garden you have, you may enjoy the maintenance and want to try different plants more often or at least seasonally. Small-leaved succulents like sedum 'Dragon's Blood' will flush out in spring and grow longer stems that eventually flower in the early summer. When new growth appears at the crown or base of a plant, it's time to shear it back. This will keep it a tighter shrub until the new growth flushes the following spring.

**WHERE TO FIND THE PLANTS** Your local garden center or nursery is a great place to start if you are just learning about miniature gardening. Plan to spend some time at the garden center looking at plants, reading tags, and getting to know plant names. Most good garden centers have staff members who are knowledgeable about miniature plants for your area. Many also have classes and workshops on beginner or container gardening for anyone brand new to the hobby. Some tried and true miniature plants to look for: small-leaved groundcovers, alpine plants, rockery plants, small-leaved sedums and succulents, miniature and dwarf plants and trees, bonsai starter plants, and slow-growing plants. Not all nurseries will be familiar with miniature garden plants so jot down this list and take it with you, just in case they start to look at you funny.

If you are ordering on the Internet, always deal with a reputable nursery. All the information you need should be in the listing, including a picture of the plant. It's always good to see what you're getting before you order it. Also be wary of ordering dormant plants online—these roots-only plants are easy to forget about if you can't see anything in the pot.

*'White Pygmy' sawara-cypress in four-inch pots, ready for sale at a nursery.*

LEFT: *Some nurseries have special areas for miniature or dwarf bedding plants.*

RIGHT: *So many miniature plants, so little time.*

## WAYS OF SEEING

By now you have hopefully caught the miniature gardening bug and are hooked for life. You'll never look at a small plant the same way again. You'll be eyeballing that low-growing anemone as a nice-sized miniature shrub and you'll single out that lone hen and chick to use as an agave plant in miniature. Remember—miniature gardening is just like full-sized gardening and there are endless ways to interpret, customize, and personalize. Miniature gardening is an excuse for adults to play, and the only hard and fast rule is to enjoy yourself.

# PLANTS FOR MINIATURE GARDENS

| BOTANICAL NAME | COMMON NAME |
| --- | --- |
| **TREES FOR SUN** | |
| *Buxus sempervirens* **'Graham Blandy'** | 'Graham Blandy' boxwood |
| *Chamaecyparis obtusa* **'Baldwin Variegated'** | 'Baldwin Variegated' dwarf hinoki cypress |
| *Chamaecyparis obtusa* **'Chirimen'** | 'Chirimen' dwarf hinoki cypress |
| *Chamaecyparis thyoides* **'Top Point'** | 'Top Point' white cedar |
| *Cryptomeria japonica* **'Tansu'** | 'Tansu' Japanese cedar |
| *Juniperus communis* **'Compressa'** | 'Compressa' juniper |
| *Juniperus communis* **'Miniature'** | 'Miniature' juniper |
| *Picea glauca* **'Pixie Dust'** | 'Pixie Dust' dwarf Alberta spruce |
| *Pinus mugo* **'Slowmound'** | 'Slowmound' mugo pine |
| *Ulmus parvifolia* **'Hokkaido'** | 'Hokkaido' dwarf princess elm |
| **SHRUBS FOR SUN** | |
| *Chameacyparis obtusa* **'Golden Sprite'** | 'Golden Sprite' dwarf hinoki cypress |
| *Chamaecyparis obtusa* **'Nana'** | 'Nana' dwarf hinoki cypress |
| *Chamaecyparis pisifera* **'White Pygmy'** | 'White Pygmy' sawara-cypress |
| *Cotoneaster integrifolius* | small-leaved cotoneaster |
| *Juniperus horizontalis* **'Mother Lode'** | 'Mother Lode' creeping juniper |
| *Picea glauca* **'Blue Planet'** | 'Blue Planet' dwarf Alberta spruce |
| *Picea glauca* **'Elf'** | 'Elf' dwarf Alberta spruce |
| *Picea glauca* **'Hobbit'** | 'Hobbit' dwarf Alberta spruce |
| *Pinus mugo* **'Michelle'** | 'Michelle' mugo pine |
| **TREES FOR SHADE** | |
| *Buxus sempervirens* **'Variegata'** | variegated English boxwood |
| *Chamaecyparis lawsoniana* **'Ellwoodii'** | 'Ellwoodii' Lawson false-cypress |
| *Cupressus macrocarpa* | Monterey cypress |
| *Euonymus japonica* **'Microphyllus Variegatus'** | variegated box-leaf euonymus |
| *Ilex crenata* **'Dwarf Pagoda'** | 'Dwarf Pagoda' Japanese holly |
| *Ilex crenata* **'Sky Pencil'** | 'Sky Pencil' Japanese holly |
| *Pieris japonica* **'Brookside Miniature'** | 'Brookside Miniature' Japanese andromeda |
| *Tsuga canadensis* **'Moon Frost'** | 'Moon Frost' Canada hemlock |
| *Tsuga canadensis* **'Jervis'** | 'Jervis' Canada hemlock |
| *Tsuga diversifolia* **'Loowit'** | 'Loowit' Japanese hemlock |

| BOTANICAL NAME | COMMON NAME |
| --- | --- |

**SHRUBS FOR SHADE**

| BOTANICAL NAME | COMMON NAME |
| --- | --- |
| *Abies koreana* **'Cis'** | 'Cis' dwarf Korean fir |
| *Abies koreana* **'Green Carpet'** | 'Green Carpet' dwarf Korean fir |
| *Buxus microphylla* **'Compacta'** | littleleaf boxwood |
| *Ilex crenata* **'Rock Garden'** | 'Rock Garden' Japanese holly |
| *Pieris japonica* **'Little Heath'** | 'Little Heath' Japanese andromeda |
| *Tsuga canadensis* **'Abbott's Pygmy'** | 'Abbott's Pygmy' Canada hemlock |
| *Tsuga canadensis* **'Hornbeck'** | 'Hornbeck' Canada hemlock |
| *Tsuga canadensis* **'Jean Iseli'** | 'Jean Iseli' Canada hemlock |

**MINIATURE BEDDING PLANTS FOR SUN**

| BOTANICAL NAME | COMMON NAME |
| --- | --- |
| *Bellium minutum* | miniature daisy |
| *Delosperma congesta* | miniature ice plant |
| *Erodium variabile* **'Flore Pleno'** | 'Flore Pleno' cranesbill |
| *Leptinella squalida* **'Platt's Black'** | 'Platt's Black' brass buttons |
| *Sedum oreganum* | Oregon stonecrop sedum |
| *Sedum spurium* | two-row stonecrop sedum |
| *Sempervivum* **species and cultivars** | hens and chicks (small cultivars) |
| *Thymus praecox* | creeping red thyme |
| *Thymus pseudolanuginosus* | woolly thyme |
| *Thymus serpyllum* **'Elfin'** | 'Elfin' thyme |

**MINIATURE BEDDING PLANTS FOR SHADE**

| BOTANICAL NAME | COMMON NAME |
| --- | --- |
| *Acorus gramineus* **'Ogon'** | 'Ogon' miniature sweet flag |
| *Cymbalaria aequitroloba* | dwarf kenilworth ivy |
| *Isotoma fluviatilis (Pratia pendunculata)* | blue star creeper |
| *Lirope spicata* | dwarf lily turf |
| *Mentha requienii* | Corsican mint |
| *Muelenbeckia complexa* | fairy vine |
| *Ophiopogon japonicus* **'Nana'** | dwarf mondo grass |
| *Saxifraga* **'Primuloides'** | 'Primuloides' miniature London pride |
| *Soleirolia soleirolii* | baby tears |
| *Soleirolia soleirolii* **'Aura'** | golden baby tears |

## IT NEEDS YOU, YOU NEED IT
### GARDEN CARE

FOR MANY, an appealing aspect of this engaging hobby is that it is as much crafting as gardening. After the initial planning and creation phases, however, gardening takes center stage. Watching how plants grow together and learning how to maintain this wee world can be as much fun as creating the garden.

*A little attention goes a long way toward keeping your miniature garden inviting.*

In this chapter, you'll learn about caring for your garden in miniature, whether it's inground or in a container. If you are a beginner, this chapter will be a helpful guide. More experienced gardeners can find new insights and ideas on caring for their miniature gardens.

## EASY CARE STARTS WITH SMART CHOICES

All plants need light, air and water; most need soil, too. If you consider these basic needs when planning your miniature garden, the care and maintenance end of things will have a good chance of going smoothly. It's also important for you to consider your time and the way you live. If you travel a lot, a miniature succulent garden is a good choice because it doesn't need regular watering. A tender, faster-growing garden welcomes regular attention.

ABOVE: *'Jean Iseli' Canada hemlock has a distinctive natural branching habit.*

BELOW: *'Butter Ball' hinoki cypress provides lovely, creamy colors.*

RIGHT: *As plants grow, it's important to snip selectively to keep elements in scale with each other.*

*A twig fence takes only minutes to install, with little ongoing maintenance.*

*Tiny flowers dot a hill of
Irish moss in midsummer.*

# INDOOR VS. OUTDOOR PLANTS

To keep plant care simple, use plants that are well suited for indoor growing conditions in indoor miniature gardens, and plants meant for outdoor growing conditions in outdoor miniature gardens. This may sound simplistic and obvious, but thinking that any plant can be grown anywhere is one of the most common mistakes new gardeners make.

Indoor plants are, for the most part, tropical plants that want to stay above sixty degrees Fahrenheit all year round. Miniature African violets, small ponytail palms, and miniature aloe vera are just a few examples of plants that need to stay warm throughout the year. In general, if you bring an outdoor plant inside, it will think it is the summer growing season all the time and grow itself to death. A plant needs periods of rest, just like us (excluding annuals and vegetables, which grow with one purpose: to produce fruit or flowers for reseeding within the season). Dry air from indoor heating can also stress outdoor plants that prefer a cool, humid environment, leaving them more susceptible to pest and disease problems.

*Saxifrages are wonderful alpine plants that prefer the outdoors.*

LEFT: *The striking yellow flowers of 'Cape Blanco' sedum add a bright accent to a miniature garden border.*

RIGHT: *Miniature daisies prefer an area with cool sun or partial shade.*

## USE THE LIGHT

Meeting the light requirements of any plant is important, because plants use light to manufacture food for themselves. Some plants need eight hours or more of full sunlight per day, while others require less. Too much sunlight on a shade plant will cause the plant leaves to burn. Too little light on a plant that needs full sun will cause the plant to reach toward the light and grow pale. The good news is that there are plants for almost every light situation—indoors and out, full shade to full sun, bright indirect light, or dappled sun. Checking the light in your chosen spot will help narrow your plant choices.

## IT'S LIGHT OUTSIDE

In the Northern Hemisphere, the south- and west-facing areas of your garden receive full sun, the east receives part or cool sun, and the north side of your garden is shaded for most of the year. In addition to the location of your garden spot, outdoor light is based upon how the sun moves through the day and through the year. Natural and manufactured sun blocks—trees and shrubs, sheds, awnings, and buildings—also affect lighting. Use the amount of sun your chosen spot gets in spring or fall to figure out what kind of light you have. With this information, you will be able to choose plants that will thrive in the conditions you have, the garden will be easier to maintain, and your plants will be happy growers. This chart will help you figure out what different kinds of light are called, often the same terms you will find in the plant's care instructions.

ABOVE: *'Blue Star' dwarf juniper thrives in full, hot sun.*

BELOW: *New needle growth on 'White Bud' mugo pine stretches toward the sun.*

# OUTDOOR LIGHT REQUIREMENTS

| SHADE AND SUN DESCRIPTIONS | DEFINITION | EXAMPLES OF SUITABLE MINIATURE AND DWARF TREES, SHRUBS, AND GROUNDCOVERS | EXAMPLES OF SUITABLE MINIATURE BEDDING PLANTS |
|---|---|---|---|
| Part shade | 2 to 4 hours of cool sun | Canada hemlock<br>littleleaf boxwood<br>Japanese holly | baby tears<br>Corsican mint |
| Full shade | Less than 2 hours of sun | Canada hemlock | golden baby tears |
| Dappled shade | A mixture of sun and shade, also called light shade or part shade | Canada hemlock<br>Japanese holly | baby tears<br>Corsican mint |
| Part sun | 4 to 6 hours of sun | balsam fir<br>littleleaf boxwood<br>hinoki cypress<br>Korean fir | dwarf mondo grass<br>fairy vine<br>groundcover thyme |
| Full sun | 6 or more hours of sun | Norway spruce<br>sawara-cypress<br>Alberta spruce<br>balsam fir | groundcover thyme<br>small-leaved sedum |
| Cool sun | Morning sun before 11:00 a.m. or after 3:00 p.m. (except in summer), or winter sun | hinoki cypress<br>Alberta spruce<br>Japanese cedar | miniature daisy<br>blue star creeper |
| Hot sun | Sun from 2:00 p.m. to 7:00 p.m. in the summertime | mugo pine<br>juniper<br>small-leaved cotoneaster | small-leaved sedum hens and chicks |

# IT'S LIGHT INSIDE

Identifying the kind of indoor light available in areas of your house generally follows the same rules as outdoor light. South- and west-facing windows are going to be the hottest. East windows will provide cool but bright light, and north windows will offer low light. If you are living in a condominium, apartment building, or urban neighborhood, your windows may be shadowed by other buildings or a neighbor's balcony for part or most of the day, calling for plants that prefer low light.

Remember that in the middle of winter, when the sun shines sideways into your east, west, or south windows, this is temporary and may only last about a month. The sun at its highest point in midsummer will not shine into your windows at all. The light in spring and autumn is most consistent; use it for planning.

The plus side of gardening indoors is that you can easily adjust for natural fluctuations by controlling the light. You can always create bright indirect light in a full-sun window by hanging a sheer curtain. You may want to move your indoor garden out of direct sun for a month or two until the light changes. The biggest threat is when the sun starts to shine directly through your windows in early autumn. That hot sunbeam can creep in unexpectedly and scorch the leaves of your miniature garden when you least expect it. To prevent this, move the garden or hang a curtain as soon as you see sunlight sneaking onto your windowsills. A strong beam of sunlight can act like Captain Kirk's laser beam in your little world, cooking whatever is in its path.

Adding more light is an easy fix, thanks to recent interest in indoor vegetable gardening. Artificial lighting opens up different areas of your home for more growing space and you can create a great growing environment almost anywhere in your home. There are many options these days for indoor grow lights, so you can either keep in mind what the plant wants and change your indoor light, or select your lighting setup first, then choose plants accordingly. Grow bulbs can also be purchased for your favorite lamp. With a small lamp and timer, you can successfully grow a garden on that dim table in the hallway.

Use the light-levels chart to figure out what light levels are already happening inside your house, or for ideas on how to create the right light to suit your plants.

# INDOOR LIGHT LEVELS

| LIGHT DESCRIPTIONS | DEFINITION | EXAMPLES OF SUITABLE MINIATURE DWARF TREES, SHRUBS AND GROUNDCOVERS | EXAMPLES OF SUITABLE MINIATURE BEDDING PLANTS |
| --- | --- | --- | --- |
| Indirect light or shade | Regular indoor lighting. A way from windows, but enough light that you are able to read a newspaper.<br><br>Northern windows. | littleleaf boxwood<br>parlor palm | African violet<br>miniature ivy |
| Bright indirect or some direct light | Beside, below, but not directly in front of east-, west-, or south- facing windows.<br><br>Behind a light/sheer curtain in a south-, east-, or west-facing window. | littleleaf boxwood<br>variegated English<br>    boxwood<br>Lawson false-cypress<br>baby ficus | drawf mondo grass<br>baby tears<br>golden baby tears<br>Corsican mint |
| Sunny | In front of east-, west-, or south- facing windows.<br><br>Plant should be able to tolerate hot, direct sun.<br><br>Some shading may be needed in midsummer. | baby jade<br>Monterey cypress<br>Buddhist pine | haworthia<br>cactus<br>succulents<br>miniature aloe vera |

## TEMPERATURE ZONES

Temperature and humidity are important considerations in your plant choices, because they directly impact your plants' health, even as much as light requirements. When you shop locally, the only plants available should be those that will grow in your climate, taking some of the research work out of your selections. Online ordering via the Internet opens up a whole new world of plant options—including plants from areas that are very unlike yours, climate-wise. You may see a plant, fall in love, and find yourself in zonal denial—that is, ignoring the fact that the plant and your environment are a poor match. Imagine planting a beautiful jade plant from a hot, humid area in a cool, temperate region, and you can see the potential for miniature garden heartbreak.

The best way to identify whether a plant is good for your chosen spot is to look for the minimum temperature on the plant's tag (which indicates how cold the weather can get before the plant will die) and match it to your climate. If only the zones are listed, look up the temperatures of that zone.

LEFT: *A young parlor palm and Norfolk Island pine in this indoor bowl garden are well-suited to the indirect light created by sheer curtains.*

RIGHT: *Irish moss is most happy in cooler zones.*

# HARDINESS ZONES

Hardiness zone charts can be very helpful in understanding the conditions in your area, but too much information can be paralyzing. Again, buy from your local nursery to benefit from their pre-selection of plants suited to your zone, or be prepared to do that research yourself when buying online. Look for temperature requirements as well as zone information.

Here is some general information on available zone charts. You may need to reference your country's zone chart to get an understanding of the zonal temperatures in your area and to memorize your hardiness zone number. Some plant tags list only the zones, not the temperatures.

**The United States Department of Agriculture** updated the USDA Plant Hardiness Zone Map in 2012 with twenty-six zones and sub-zones. This is the most popular reference chart among American gardeners, and it's based on average minimum winter temperature. Their interactive map is available online, where you can enter your zip code and get your exact zone immediately, at

    http://www.usna.usda.gov/Hardzone/ ushzmap.html

**Canada's National Land and Water Information Service** has divided the country into seventeen major zones and sub-zones. With a wider range of climates, the zones take into account the minimum winter temperatures, the length of the frost-free period, the amount of rain throughout the year, maximum temperatures, wind speeds, and snow cover. Zones for Canada can be found at

    http://sis.agr.gc.ca/cansis/nsdb/climate/ hardiness/intro.html

**In the United Kingdom** zone information can be found at

    http://www.gardeningzone.org/content/ content.php/hardiness-zones-uk/

**For Europe,** see

    http://uk.gardenweb.com/forums/ zones/hze.html

Again, please refer to your country's agricultural department for more information on your specific growing zones. If all of this research feels overwhelming, simply compare your local temperatures to the requirements listed on the tag or in the plant listing. That's all you really need to know, and you can always come back for a more in-depth analysis at a later date.

LEFT: *Snow-covered miniature gardens have a beauty all their own—but make sure your plants can take the cold!*

RIGHT: *The evergreens in this scene suggest a mountain locale.*

## BRINGING THE OUTSIDE IN

You can bring your outdoor miniature garden inside for a few days at a time in the winter to use for a centerpiece, for example, but it should be placed outside to rest afterwards, and watered thoroughly until it drains out the bottom. The time the garden spends outside should be greater than the time it spends inside—the trick is to not let it acclimate to the indoor environment. While inside, your outdoor miniature garden soil should remain damp and not be left to dry out. Avoid direct sunlight when your garden is in its temporary place inside too, as the soil may dry out too fast and plant leaves could get scorched.

Never move a garden immediately from a warm room to the frosty outdoors, or from a shaded room to full, hot, outdoor sun, without first staging it in the garage or on a covered porch for at least a couple of days. The purpose of staging is to help the garden adapt to the change in environment slowly and gradually, and to avoid shocking the plants with extreme climate changes. For best results, choose a staging spot with light and temperatures that are in between the outdoor and indoor environments.

## SOIL BASICS

Soil is another major factor affecting plant growth and health. Soil is alive. Dirt is dead. You can see the difference. Soil is dark, rich, and full of organic matter. It contains earthworms, fungi, tiny insects, and other living creatures. Dirt is the gray grit between the cracks in the sidewalk. Just as plants have different light and temperature preferences, they also have varied soil requirements. Succulents need a sandier, fast-draining soil, while many conifers need a loamy soil to help keep their roots damp.

*Full-sized soil rules apply to tiny worlds as well.*

*This tiny, ornate pot requires the right soil to successfully grow* Sedum album.

**SOIL IN THE OUTDOOR GARDEN BED** If you are new to gardening and want to plant an inground miniature garden in an outdoor bed, check with your local nursery for their soil recommendations. Bring in a sample; they should be able to tell you how to amend it, if needed. If you would like more details about the soil before you plant, the nursery should be able to have it tested, or you can find an online resource to send it to. You can improve soil by simply adding something (sand, compost, manure, or more topsoil) to get a good balance of nutrition for the roots and drainage for the water. Amending the soil will improve it naturally, and it is the best way to start a miniature inground garden. Do not think a bottle of fertilizer will make dirt into soil—it will not.

As you delve further into gardening, you may soon realize there are many microclimates and different growing conditions within your own backyard. One area may have sandy soil, while nearby the soil is more clay-like. If you don't know what you have, ask a neighbor who gardens. Gardeners love to tell you what you don't know, so don't be shy about asking!

LEFT: *Good potting soil will help keep this sedum rooting healthy.*

RIGHT: *Fast-draining, sandy soil will make any cactus happy in its container.*

## HOW BIG, HOW MANY, HOW MUCH?

| POT WIDTH | NUMBER OF TREES | NUMBER OF GROUNDCOVER STARTS | SOIL (approximate) |
| --- | --- | --- | --- |
| Less than 5 inches | 0 | 1 | 4 quarts |
| 5 to 6 inches | 0 | 1 or 2 | 6 quarts |
| 6 to 8 inches | 1 | 1 | 8 quarts |
| 8 to 11 inches | 1 to 2 | 2 | 14 quarts |
| 11 to 14 inches | 2 or 3 | 2 or 3 | 1 cubic foot |

**SOIL FOR CONTAINER GARDENING** For container gardening, the soil from your garden bed will not work. It is usually too heavy and doesn't have the right balance of nutrients for a contained environment. Potting soil has sufficient space for air and water, as well as nutrients that are engineered to provide everything a plant needs to stay healthy inside its container. Some plants need particular types of soil mixes to manage water absorption and provide what they need to survive. This information is usually noted within the plant's care instructions.

A dry-garden cactus does not have the same soil needs as a moisture-loving African violet. The cactus likes water to drain quickly from the soil, and would prefer to stay on the dry side—so adding extra drainage material (sand, vermiculite, or perlite) to the potting mix will keep water away from soil around the roots. African violets, on the other hand, prefer to stay a little moist. They don't mind sitting in a shallow saucer of water for days and prefer extra loam or peat in the soil to help retain moisture around the roots.

Beware of potting soil that includes fertilizer. This type of soil is meant for annuals and vegetables, and is not ideal for miniature gardens. After all, we want plants to stay small and grow slowly—fertilizer works against that objective.

Generic or less expensive potting soil mixes may need extra drainage material. Once again, soil amendments like perlite or vermiculite will improve the flow of water through the soil. This will help ensure that the plant's roots are not constantly wet—a condition that causes many plants to rot and die. Check your local nursery or garden center for these items.

Use the chart above to help figure out how much soil you need. If plants are chosen correctly, a miniature garden planted at least eight inches deep and wide will easily last for years without repotting.

## PLANTS AND WATER

Water preferences should also be considered when choosing plants, especially if your miniature garden is in a container. Different plants have different watering needs, but plants in the same garden should all tolerate the same watering schedule. Some plants like their root zone to dry out between waterings; others like to have a moist root zone at all times—planting these varieties next to each other in a small container can result in disaster. This chart explains terms usually found on the plant tag, or in the plant's description.

The only way to really test a plant's thirst is to put your finger down at least one inch into the soil and feel how wet it is. Many types of water meters are available that you can poke into the soil, but they are not always reliable. The best indicator is how the soil feels; the second best is how it looks. Dry soil is lighter in color and will eventually pull away from the sides of the pot. Moist soil is deep in color and looks full and rich. Soil that is too wet looks black and develops a slimy film on the surface.

*Sedums and succulents*
*need good drainage to keep*
*the soil on the dry side.*

## WATER NEEDS

| | MEANING | EXAMPLE |
|---|---|---|
| Wet | The plant pot sits in a shallow dish of water, or is in a container (cache pot) without drainage, and the soil is kept wet | African violets miniature sweet flag |
| Moist | Pot has a drainage hole, but is watered often to keep up the moisture level | begonias baby tears |
| Damp | Watered regularly, but soil is allowed to almost dry out in between, like a wrung-out sponge. | Lawson false-cypress variegated English boxwood |
| Dry | Soil is allowed to dry out a completely between waterings. | succulents cactus |

## CATCHING THE WATER

Saucers placed under a pot are ideal to catch and control excess water where you need to, but it is best to avoid them outdoors. In some circumstances they are necessary, such as condo and apartment balconies where the water would drip onto your neighbor's balcony below. Use pot feet to raise the container off the balcony or deck floor and put a small saucer underneath, centering the saucer under drainage holes to catch runoff. Empty it often or the pot will be sitting in stagnant water, keeping the soil inside too wet.

For indoor miniature gardens, if your pot did not come with a matching saucer, your local nursery will provide a number of options. Clear plastic saucers come in many sizes, and will fit into any décor or theme. Choose a saucer that is at least a half inch bigger than the pot on all sides so the water will have a place to go. A snug-fitting saucer might look better, but will not work very well in collecting extra water.

Never trust any saucer on your good wood surfaces. Even ceramic saucers that have been fired and glazed in high-temperature kilns can still absorb moisture and wick the dampness through to the surface beneath. Also beware of condensation when growing plants indoors; over time the dampness can affect a wood finish dramatically.

Choose the best solutions available at your local nursery or garden center so you can place your miniature garden where you want. Cork or felt mats with plastic backs work well as long as they stay dry. If you overwater and the saucer overflows, you run the risk of soaking this protective mat, too. Always check containers and saucers after watering to prevent this, or put the pot in the sink to drain before placing it back on the saucer.

LEFT: *Raindrops on a dwarf Alberta spruce.*

RIGHT: *A small visitor checks out the dark depths of a miniature pond feature.*

*Whether as a feature or as sustenance, water is an essential part of every garden.*

*Even the smallest containers often come with a water-catching saucer.*

# FOOD AND FERTILIZING

Feeding your miniature garden is not necessary on any regular basis because you simply don't want the plants to grow fast. Your goal is to keep the garden growing and weaving together for as long as possible—hopefully for a couple of years, or until you feel the need to switch it around and try something new. The plants you choose will also factor into the feeding schedule. Good examples are dwarf and miniature conifers; when planted in a garden bed, they don't need any fertilizer, but after growing in a pot for more than a few years, they will need a bit of feeding. Fresh potting soil usually has enough nutrients for the first couple of years, then you can start using a time-release organic fertilizer in the spring and mid-summer. Plant fertilizer comes in granular form. Sprinkle it on top of the soil around the plant, like you would pepper a tomato, then use a fork (garden or dinner, depending on your garden's size) to till it into the soil.

Understanding the basics of light, soil, and water requirements will allow you to consider these important factors when selecting plants for your miniature garden. Designing with plant care needs in mind will make tending your garden simple and keep your plants happy and healthy. If you are brand new to gardening, choose a couple of plants to start with, grow them until you are comfortable with the watering and maintenance routine, then gradually try out more ideas and plants as your confidence grows. Try to resist going nuts on your first trip to the nursery, though the many options make it tempting to buy more than you need. Instead, start a sketchbook or a journal to jot down your all your plant and garden ideas—they will wait for you.

LEFT: *After a couple of years, your miniature plants may need a bit of fertilizer to maintain good health.*

RIGHT: *Careful watering will keep this garden flourishing.*

## PERSONALITY PLUS
MINIATURE GARDEN
ACCESSORIES

ONCE YOU ADD a miniature garden accessory to your pot of plants, the scene suddenly shrinks down to scale, the pebble mulch turns into a mini patio area, and you have a fanciful, living scene. A true garden in miniature needs at least one tiny accessory. Whether it's a small bench, a birdhouse, or something decorative, these focal points are key signals that something magical is afoot.

*Well-chosen accents and accessories tell a story about your miniature garden.*

A realistic miniature garden accessory creates an illusion. If you didn't know better, you'd swear that garden bench or birdbath is full-sized, just waiting for a person or bird to enter the scene. You then see the garden's plants and patio as miniatures, too, and the scene is complete. As long as the accessory is realistic, you can rely on it to cinch the scene. This attention to accessory detail and authenticity is what creates the enchantment—that "Ahhhh!" moment—of a successful miniature garden. Only the context of the environment outside the garden tells you it's a trick of the eye. But within that play between life size and miniature scale lies a world brimming with delight and imagination.

ABOVE: *Who wouldn't want to take a break from the worries of the world in this peaceful spot?*

BELOW: *Animal accessories quickly shrink a garden's scale and provide important focal points.*

*This small-scale farmstead is packed with engaging points of interest.*

## DOES IT BELONG?

With the multitude of miniature accessories out there, the best question to ask when choosing items for your garden is an easy one: would they be there in real life? If they don't belong in your life-sized garden, they likely won't work in a miniature garden, either.

A blazing pink, plastic elephant, fun as it is, tends to monopolize the viewer's eye, not to mention seeming incongruous with the scene and scale. Is it supposed to represent a real animal, or a garden statue? Painting the elephant to resemble concrete or wood conveys that it is merely garden art and clears up the confusion. The faster the brain accepts the idea, the quicker the illusion succeeds, turning the moment into one of whimsy and fun.

Not only is the accessory's perceived or actual medium important for realism, its size is crucial too. Make sure all of your garden art, accessories, and patio materials are the same scale, and realistically placed in the miniature garden scene. Even a single item of a slightly different scale will seem out of place, confusing the viewer and spoiling the impact. The ideas are indeed limitless, but if you replicate or mimic materials that are used in full-sized gardens, your chances of succeeding are much greater.

Above all, have fun exploring the ways a figure or ornament can transform the personality of your garden. If it looks good to you and puts a smile on your face, then you have done it perfectly.

LEFT: *An amphibious bronze sentry watches over this miniature garden.*

RIGHT: *This gardener's corner is filled with true-to-life accessories, in perfect scale to each other.*

# HOW IMPORTANT IS QUALITY?

Collectors spend thousands on intricate handmade miniatures, but these are obviously not meant for the living garden. At the opposite end of the spectrum are inexpensive trinkets that won't last long in the garden or elsewhere. Wise miniature gardeners know how to weigh cost and craftsmanship to select accessories that will add a priceless accent to their gardens without overspending.

If your garden will be outdoors, remember that colors fade in the sun, wind wreaks havoc, and wood expands and contracts with the moisture in the air. Any kind of paper, including cardboard, will be destroyed with the first rain. Weather happens, right along with other unpredictable events—squirrels foraging, cats chasing birds, and dogs being dogs. In the case of outdoor gardens, quality means hardy materials and construction that will stand up to the elements, whether those elements are a rare hailstorm or your neighbor's three-year-old playing Godzilla.

Indoor gardens offer a little more room for indulgence. Here, quality can mean personal treasures—perhaps your grandmother's tiny handmade rocking chair or an artist's diminutive masterpiece. If your indoor garden will be sharing space with young children or pets, however, you'll have to take steps to protect all from harm.

The dollhouse industry offers a wealth of possibilities for miniature gardeners. Most pieces are of a quality that is ideal for indoor gardens and offer some durability for outdoor use. In general, if you decide to make miniature gardening a serious hobby, invest in products that will hold up over time. And keep this caution in mind: If you can't afford to lose it, don't use it.

LEFT: *A rustic picket fence creates a yard-like effect.*

RIGHT: *Wood lends authenticity to architectural elements.*

*Weather-vulnerable items like books and pillows should be taken inside for the winter.*

*Popular Adirondack styling is available in a range of miniature furniture pieces.*

# NOT-SO-HEAVY METAL

Whether painted a bold color or rusted and aged, metal or faux metal is a welcome addition to the garden. Scaled down to miniature, a traditional metal arbor straddling a tiny pathway between dwarf conifers can be both enchanting and realistic. A white metal wicker settee at the bottom of a miniature garden path is so inviting, you'll want to drink Alice's elixir, grab a book, and camp out for a day.

If your metal garden accessory has begun rusting, and you don't like the look, sand down all rust spots with fine sandpaper until the rust is completely gone. Spray it with a sealer, then spray with a metal rustproof paint. This may have to be done annually; once metal has rusted, the rust is hard to get rid of completely. But you can stay on top of the process by keeping the metal sealed from air and moisture, checking often, and treating it promptly when rust appears. This kind of project is great for those winter days where you would rather be outside, but can at least dream and scheme while tending to your miniature accessories.

You can make just about anything look like metal these days with metallic paints and specialized finishes. Bronze and verdigris finishes need to be protected with polyurethane to make them sunproof. Rust paint also works well when applied correctly. These treatments can be used on faded accessories, too, giving them new life and keeping them out of the landfill. Always use your least favorite accessory, or an odd toy, to test and perfect the process first.

LEFT: *A tumbled column gives the impression of ruins from long ago.*

RIGHT: *Metal or metal-look accents contrast with the organic nature of plants.*

# PLASTIC BUT PERMANENT

Many wonderful things are happening with resin these days. Although it is a plastic and will unfortunately not biodegrade, it is strong, sunproof, and rainproof. The level of detail captured with this medium is comparable to that of wood carving— at a fraction of the cost. Anything made of resin weathers very well, can easily be drilled and staked to keep its place in the garden soil, can be brought in for a good scrub with soap and water when dirty, and is repaired easily. Stained resin will hold its color in direct sun, too.

A broad range of resin garden statuary, urns, and furniture is available. Traditional figures such as St. Francis of Assisi, Flora the Goddess of Spring, or even Michelangelo's David come in resin and can be glued to a pedestal for a dramatic presence in your tiny landscape. Miniature Roman or ancient urns, Victorian birdbaths, faux stone animal statues, or a petite gazing ball on a tiny pedestal can also add charm to the scene. Benches that seem made of stone come in a variety of scales. Brick-like walls, antique fountains, and birdbaths decorated with twirling grapevine tendrils are all available in a durable resin that will wear well in an outdoor garden scene.

Plastic accents such as garden gnomes, Buddha figures, pink flamingos, and animals of all kinds are great in a miniature garden. If used outdoors, brightly colored accessories will need to be treated so they don't fade in the sun; a quick application of acrylic UV spray twice a year will keep the hues fresh and vivid.

If your wee accessory has faded over time, resin can easily accept a wash of acrylic paint to spruce it up. Broken pieces can be easily repaired with crazy glue or two-part epoxy and painted for a second life.

LEFT: *Whimsical garden art adds color and interest.*

RIGHT: *The canopy of a miniature wisteria provides welcome shade.*

# WOOD ACCESSORIES, FENCES, AND TRELLISES

Wood is a natural fit in any garden. Bare wood will age and weather. As it expands and contracts with air moisture, painted wood will eventually fade and flake. Stained wood will slow down the sun's bleaching process, but you may have to restain at least once a year to keep it looking fresh.

You can also paint your faded wood accessories to give them new life. A small set of acrylic paints goes a long way in the miniature garden studio. Washes of color can add up to an aged and antique look—or a thick coat of paint can make a dated accessory appear new. Just give the piece a little sanding to make sure it's free of dirt, and be sure to let it dry thoroughly between coats.

ABOVE: *A well-loved back patio, miniature-style.*

FAR RIGHT: *Architectural elements make a statement in miniature.*

BELOW: *Unconventional accents give this wood chair an eclectic flair.*

# TAKE A SEAT WITH GARDEN FURNITURE

The addition of garden furniture to your wee world can elegantly complete a vignette. Since it's such a familiar part of our full-sized world, furniture also conveys scale quickly. A simple garden bench under a tree, or a solitary chair on the patio, can transport you to a different place and time instantly.

A patio set is equally enchanting, especially if there are small personal effects, such as a miniature book or a garden hat. Your imagination starts to fill in the blanks. A half-inch scale table, not even two inches tall, with two tiny chairs, creates a very sweet miniature setting. A one-inch patio set with a table and four chairs leaves room for family and friends to join you. One comfy chair in a partially hidden corner implies a special hideaway.

Lounge chairs, settees, rocking chairs, twig chairs, benches, and love seats can communicate different messages and moods. With your choices and arrangement of furniture, you can convey relaxation, contentment, whimsy, or togetherness.

*A seat for two creates a perfect garden spot for reading or daydreaming.*

# BUILD A MOOD WITH MINIATURE STRUCTURES

Structures in the garden are larger accessories such as trellises, fences, bridges, wishing wells, or walls and panels. Some settings feature buildings—garden sheds or cabins. At full size, they are usually hard to move, so you plant around them. In miniature, there are many kinds of structures you can add to your garden quickly and easily—and best of all, you don't have to bribe your neighbor to help move them.

Most miniature garden structures are available in large size or one-inch scale. When placed as they would be in a full-sized garden, they can add an extra layer of realism.

Some structures, like a wishing well or fence, can be easily added without disturbing plants, yet can instantly change the theme of your garden. A wishing well can look right at home between shrubs, with perhaps a path leading to it. Fences can easily line a patio or pathway, or they can rim the outside of the pot or border.

Structures like arbors or bridges require a bit of pre-planning to look right. An arbor could arch over a pathway or shelter a bench at the bottom of a path. A miniature bridge over a dry riverbed provides the perfect hiding place for a wee gnome.

Gazebos, fairy houses, and more are available in miniature. Just be careful to select items of the same scale. A half-inch scale bench will look lost in a one-inch scale gazebo. A one-inch scale birdbath will tower over a tiny quarter-inch scale bench. Note that when you put a house in the garden it pulls the eye away from the garden, and the house becomes the focal point of the miniature scene.

LEFT: *Worn green paint ties together a garden love seat, table, and wheelbarrow.*

RIGHT: *A miniature bentwood rocker is the star of this patio.*

# MINIATURE GARDEN TOOLS AND PATIO EQUIPMENT

Miniature tools and equipment can add a lot of fun to your setting. Tiny hand tools, shovels, rakes, potting benches, wheelbarrows, and lawnmowers can all help with the theme. A straw hat on a bench next to a small bucket of garden tools is a peaceful garden scene. A rusted lawnmower in a pot full of long grass can make a fun joke gift. Find these types of replica tools at your favorite miniature store.

The smaller the miniature garden accessories get, the more apt you are to lose them. Gather tiny hand tools into a miniature trug or bucket, use a tall pot to corral your rake, shovel, and hoe, and stand them up against a miniature tree. A little silicone glue can hold that hat down on the garden bench so it doesn't fly off when a squirrel scurries through. (Honestly, they don't remember where they bury their nuts, so it is a random search every day.)

Barbecues, fire pits, and all kinds of tiny pots and urns can unleash countless opportunities for fun. Take it one step further and get some food to barbecue. Find stumps, twigs, or driftwood for the fire pit. Use sedum cuttings and plant the tiny pots with living plants.

*Miniature doesn't get much more authentic than this well-used lawn mower, complete with a handy can of lubricant.*

LEFT: *Save leftover bricks and terracotta pieces to help with the garden's realism.*

RIGHT: *Even the smallest garden deserves a set of tools.*

## GARDEN STATUARY

Statuary is a fancy word for statues; a statue is a sculpture that represents a human or an animal. In the garden center world, it refers to anything cast in stone or iron. By simply adding a single statue or urn, you can change the whole tone of your miniature scene. A statue of the Madonna or Buddha can turn the setting into a miniature grotto or altar. Any classic sculptures or large urns can instantly give your garden a European flair.

The scale of the sculpture can be flexible, as full-sized statues come in all sizes. But do try to make sure the piece is somewhat in proportion to the garden. A tiny sculpture of David in a large inground mini garden would get lost; he would do better on the patio of a mid-sized container garden. An eight-inch-tall bather sculpture would be ideal next to an inground garden pond.

Staking small sculptures is usually necessary because of the columnar shape and narrow base that the little figure stands on, which normally does not offer much of an anchor. You can stake accessories easily by drilling a hole at least a quarter of an inch deep into the bottom of the accessory and use two-part epoxy to keep the metal rod in place.

## GETTING ARTSY

Using abstract miniature garden art can be tricky. If you wouldn't normally see it in a garden, there's nothing from real life for the eye to compare it with, and the sense of scaling down—along with the illusion—is lost. If you choose to go abstract, place a bench or other recognizable accessory somewhere in the scene so there is an access point for the viewer to identify that it is a miniature scene.

## THE ANIMAL KINGDOM

Animals add an entertaining dimension to any garden, and for a miniature scene, you can include them in more ways than one. The toy and dollhouse industries provide us with many realistic four-legged miniatures to use in the garden. Pets and farm animals are plentiful, and the selection is quite wide. For jungle, forest, and desert animals, check toy or craft stores. Plastic dinosaurs and all kinds of fish are available if you are doing a prehistoric or underwater theme. The quality of these items has been improved over the last few years and it is no longer difficult to find pieces with nice detailing and precise painting.

By changing the color of the miniature animal, you can turn it into garden art. Paint it verdigris, bronze, or rust, and dedicate it to a favorite pet. Mount it on a pedestal for added effect.

LEFT: *Topping a garden-in-a-milk-pail with a Holstein dairy cow adds a wink and some whimsy.*

RIGHT: *Everything in this scene has a familiar life-sized counterpart, so the illusion is easily achieved.*

*One of the forest's smaller residents makes his way out of the pond.*

*A carved wood fawn gives viewers good reason to give the garden a closer look.*

## WATER FEATURES

Water and plants are a natural fit, capturing a soothing sense of refreshment. Creating them in miniature significantly reduces the complexity, time, price, and maintenance typically involved in full-sized water features.

Design additions can be as involved as a small waterfall or as simple as a birdbath. Creating a natural-looking water feature will add another level of expertise to your bag of miniature gardening tricks. Lakes can be installed right in the garden bed; ponds can go in a small pot. Be sure to match the scale of a lake or pond with the surrounding plants. A good rule of thumb is the rule of thirds—make the lake one-third the size of the container and plantings can take up two-thirds of the space, or vice-versa. A pond can be smaller.

Have fun with the shape of the lake or pond pot. Or create only a section of lake, where water comes right up to the edge of the container, looking like a slice taken out of a bigger scene. Create your own beach vacation or a favorite fishing spot.

### Fountains and Waterfalls

A real fountain or waterfall can be a fabulous addition to an inground miniature garden. To help ensure success, look for the smallest pump possible. The size of the pump is described in gallons per hour or gph. The more gallons pumped, the bigger the pump—most are just too big for a miniature garden. The smallest pump available is thirty-five gph and measures a little over two inches square. The smaller the pump, the more fussy it will be about particles of soil clogging the filter; maintenance can be a challenge. Bring your patience and be prepared for some tinkering.

Small, tabletop fountains are available today that are excellent options for miniature gardens. These self-contained focal points are very easy to maintain; the pump is integrated and can be refilled easily from the top of the fountain. If you would like to include a fountain in your miniature garden, purchase the fountain before the pot, so that you know it will fit into your scene. Fountains can often be found in gift or home stores, or specialty boutiques. Follow the instructions carefully. Note that tabletop fountains are meant for indoor use and if used outside, may have to be sheltered from the rain.

LEFT: *Creating a realistic shoreline requires some planning.*

RIGHT: *Not all water features require water. Tumbled glass is a lovely representation.*

## CHANGING PERSONALITIES

Most miniature gardeners like to keep an array of accessories on hand. When friends or family members drop by, you can switch out a piece for something they'll appreciate, or that will make them laugh. For visitors who are less enthusiastic about miniature gardening, this is a fun way to see if they notice changes. You can tailor the garden to theme parties, special anniversaries, or honored guests this way—and it gives you another excuse to play with your miniature garden.

*Expecting guests who love surprises? Give them something fun to discover.*

## WOULD YOU DO THAT AT HOME?

With literally thousands of accessories available, it can be hard to rein in shopping impulses. As noted, it's nice to have a collection of pieces from which to choose and swap out accessories when needed. However, resist the urge to overload a garden with incongruous items, or to place them in unrealistic settings. Ask yourself, "Would I do this in my full-sized garden?" If the answer is no, err on the side of restraint. Less is more when recreating realism.

*Pink flamingos are perfect for a festive occasion.*

ABOVE LEFT: *A bountiful holiday feast awaits.*

BELOW: *Swap the bench in your garden for a red settee and you're on your way to a holiday scene.*

CENTER: *With a few tiny ornaments, bows, and gifts, your garden is in the spirit of the season.*

RIGHT: *Beware all who dare to pass: this Halloween garden may be bewitched.*

# THROUGH THE SEASONS AND BEYOND

The options for playing with your miniature garden are endless, but it's especially fun to customize scenes to celebrate the changing seasons, special occasions, and holidays. Create a miniature garden centerpiece for Thanksgiving dinner. A tiny, four-inch garden is an inexpensive but memorable hostess gift for holiday parties. A wedding-themed scene can be part of the décor for a bridal shower. Themes can spring from anything: personal or cultural history, fairy tales, movies, or books. If you can think it, you can do it.

# LET'S MAKE
# SOME MAGIC

## MINIATURE GARDEN
## PROJECTS

CREATING YOUR OWN little world is a lot of fun once you have the right parts, plants, and pieces all together. So collect the ingredients and tools, pour a favorite beverage, and enjoy some creative time with your new hobby.

*Dwarf conifers, small-leaved shrubs, and natural accents give this setting a woodsy feel.*

# A TINY GARDEN IN A POT

A GREAT INTRODUCTION to miniature gardening, this project takes only an afternoon to create and covers the foundation steps for most small-scale container gardens. From these basics, you can go larger or smaller and add or subtract features or plants in future gardens. The plants should be able to stay in this container and grow together for a couple of years before needing any repotting or dividing.

## MATERIALS

Pot, 11 inches wide and deep

2 dwarf trees, 1 tall, 1 medium height, in 4-inch pots

3 different groundcovers or small-leaved plants, in 4-inch pots

Potting soil

## TOOLS AND SUPPLIES

Gloves (optional)

Knife

*Green on green works in this monochromatic indoor garden in a glazed pot.*

## A TINY GARDEN IN A POT

**1.**

Choose the best side of the container; that will be the front of the garden. Fill the container with potting soil until it is almost full. Ground level should be, at most, a half inch below the rim of the pot. Gently tap the plastic nursery pots off the trees and loosen the roots with your fingers.

If the roots are tightly compacted and you are unable to loosen them easily, carefully use a knife to score them every inch or so around the root balls. This will signal the roots that there is new soil to grow into. If only a few roots are showing, just plant as is.

**2.**

If the plants can be divided, gently pull the root ball apart and place the divisions to balance the design. Place trees in the back corner or rear of the pot, best sides facing frontward. Create a small hole for each root ball; the crown of the root mass should be at ground level. If a hole is too deep, lift the plant slightly and tuck soil underneath.

Tap the pots off the groundcovers, loosen the roots, and place them according to your design. All plants should be at the same ground level.

**3.**

Fill gaps in between plants and the pot, as well as between each plant. Pack the soil in gently to avoid air pockets. Tuck soil between the plants by carefully lifting the leaves up with one hand, while poking more soil in with the other hand, until the garden bed is filled in.

**4.**

Gently push the whole bed towards the back of the pot to clear space for your patio. This cleared area should be 1 inch to 1¼ inches deeper than ground level, depending on the depth of your patio material. The bottom ¾ inch of the cleared area will be filled with a layer of sand, then mini patio mix. When the patio is done, it should be even with the surrounding ground, so adjust the cleared depth accordingly, leaving enough room for the thickness of your patio material, stones, or tiles. Create the S or U shape of your garden bed from your chosen design. Even out the soil in the future patio area and tamp down gently to eliminate any air pockets.

# YOUR CUSTOM MINIATURE PATIO

## MATERIALS

Dry mini patio mix, about 1 pound

Sand, ½ pound

Patio materials: ½ pound tile pieces, small stone sheet

Border edging, 1-foot length

Wood skewers

Miniature garden accessories: bench, hanging pot with shepherd's hook

Sedum cutting

## TOOLS AND SUPPLIES

Gloves (optional)

Hand clippers

Scissors

Water sprayer with a mist setting

## YOUR CUSTOM MINIATURE PATIO

**1.**

Cut a little off the end of your border material to follow the inside curve of the pot so that you have a snug fit—whether it is straight, curved, or slanted. This will keep the dry patio mix from washing into the garden bed when it is misted with water at the end of the project. Hold the cut end of the border edging where you want it on the inside of the pot. Use a skewer to help hold it in place, while bending the border against the edge of the garden bed and across to the other side, butting up against the other side of the pot. Note or mark with your fingers where you want to make the second cut, then cut the border edging a little longer than the mark.

**2.**

Put the border edging back in the pot using the skewers to help keep it in place. If it doesn't fit, take it out and shave more off the end gradually. Be sure the border butts up against both sides of the pot and fits against the garden bed. Place skewers in the corners to hold the border firm. Place a third skewer to hold the middle bend or curve, creating a firm and level garden edge. The top of the border edging should be level with the top of the pot. Fill in both sides of the border with soil to help keep it in place, too. Your miniature garden is now ready for the patio. Don't water the plants now—the *soil in the patio area must be dry* before you move on to the next step.

**3.**

Top off the patio area with more dry potting soil, leaving at least 1 inch from the top of the border edge. Level the surface all around the patio area by adding more soil if needed. Tamp lightly to make sure there are no air holes in the soil. Pour sand into the contained area, about ¼ inch deep. This sand base will buffer the dry mini patio mix from the soil and roots. Smooth out the sand until even throughout the patio area. Gently push some into the corners. Pour a pile of dry mini patio mix into the contained area. Smooth out mix until even throughout the area. Make this layer about ½ inch deep.

**4.**

Lay out the patio pieces or tiles on the table so you can see the different shapes and sizes. Get your cobblestone pebbles or your pebble sheet ready, too. If you are putting a pathway in the middle or around the edges as shown, lay this in first, then work around it with the patio stones. Think of it as a jigsaw puzzle and start with the corners first. Place them gently, working from one side to the other, adjusting pieces for the best fit. Tops of the stones should be level with each other and the pot's edge. If a tile fits perfectly on two sides but leaves a large gap on the other side, try another piece. The gaps between stones should be consistent across the patio for a realistic look.

As you lay the pieces in, place your hand flat on top to see if they are level with each other, with the garden border, and with the pot's edge. Keep checking; if a stone is too low, gently lift it up, add a little patio mix beneath it, lay it back down, and check again.

**5.**

When you are finished laying in all the stones, gently tamp them down with a flat piece of wood or one of the unused tile pieces. This will level the tops of the stones in relation to each other, to create a smooth surface.

**6.**

Gently pour a small pile of dry mini patio mix onto the middle of your patio stones. Be careful not to pour it into the garden, using your other hand as a barrier. Then with a flat hand, smooth the mixture into the spaces, corners, and edges of the patio between stones. Carefully tap the pot on its side to settle the stones and mix, and to eliminate any air pockets. Check the surface again to ensure that all stones are level with each other. Add more patio mix if needed.

## YOUR CUSTOM MINIATURE PATIO

**7.**

Using caution—the edges of the tile, marble, or glass pieces may be sharp—gently sweep off the excess patio mix with your hand and return leftover mix to the bag for future use. Take care not to disturb the stones. If some mix gets into the garden bed, clean it out later when the patio has cured awhile, so as not to upset the work already done. You can remove the skewers gently if they are not holding the border in place any longer; fill in the skewer holes with more mix. If the border edging still needs to be held in place, cut the skewer in half and bury it just beneath the patio surface. Don't fuss with the garden bed at this point, to avoid getting soil mixed up with the patio mix.

**8.**

Using the finest mist setting on your water sprayer, lightly mist the patio from one side to the other. Wash the stones and wet down the dry mix as you work across the patio. Stop when the water starts to pool on the patio surface. Wait to brush off sand or excess mix until after the patio has cured— otherwise, the texture will be ruined and it won't look real. Water plants gently but thoroughly from the back side of the garden bed.

Let your patio cure slowly. The slower it cures, the stronger it will be. If you have made your patio in a movable container, place the pot in a shady spot for a couple of days so the patio doesn't dry out too quickly. If your patio is in a sunny garden bed, cover it with plastic (a plastic bag is fine) and keep the plastic in place with wood skewers or rocks, for at least one day. Mist the patio often throughout the first day to slow the curing process.

**9.**

Your patio will set up within a few hours, but curing takes longer. Treat the area gently during this period, keeping it damp and out of the sun for at least twenty-four hours. After that, you can add accessories to complete the scene. Wait at least a month or two if you want to move the whole patio to a different location.

## Patio repair

If there are gaps or cracks in your patio, let the area dry completely, then sprinkle some dry mini patio mix in the gaps, sweep off the excess, and mist with water.

*Once cured, your patio is ready for accessories.*

# A PEBBLE PATIO IN THE GARDEN BED

PEBBLES CAN ADD beautiful texture and color to miniature gardens, whether they are the sole material in a small patio, or define a path through the middle of a garden bed. A pebble patio is also simpler and quicker to create than a permanent one—something many enthusiasts appreciate. There are countless types and colors of pebbles, so don't be afraid to experiment and take full advantage of your range of options.

## MATERIALS

Border edging, 2 feet

Wood skewers, 4

Small pebbles, about 2 pounds

Landscape cloth, about 12 inches by
    12 inches

## TOOLS AND SUPPLIES

Gloves (optional)

Trowel

Scissors

Kneeling pad

Miniature garden furniture

*Small pebbles make for a simple yet sophisticated patio.*

## A PEBBLE PATIO

**1.**

 In the area where you want to build your patio, clear debris and carve out the soil about 1 inch deep.

**2.**

 Line the perimeter of the carved area with border edging, using skewers to hold it in place. The border edging will corral the pebbles so they don't get scattered about in the garden bed. Work from one side to the other, making sure the border is level. Cut off any extra material. Add or remove soil so the area is 1 inch deep and level. Fill in the back side of the border—the garden bed side—with soil, bringing it just below the top edge of the border.

**3.**

Place the landscape cloth over the patio area, lining up one of the sides with the edge of the cloth. Hold it in place while you cut around the edge of the patio area, using the border as a guide for the scissors. (You won't be able to see the border, but you can feel it with the lower blade of the scissors.) Landscape cloth under the stones keeps them clean, so your miniature patio will look like new for years. When it's time for a change, the clean stones can be easily recovered and reused. Instead of landscape cloth, you can use mesh screen or burlap—both make ideal barriers while letting water through.

**4.**
Pour pebbles gently into the prepared area. Smooth these into the corners and pat them down so they are level. A depth of 1 inch is ideal for pebble patios.

**5.**
Place your accessories. (Then brag about installing a garden patio in less than an hour.)

Create a charming outdoor room.

# A SECRET GARDEN

THIS LOVELY CONTAINER garden has lots of greenery, including a dwarf tree and a variety of shrubs and groundcovers. Our project adds a delightful surprise—a tiny path leading to a secret garden. Like all good secret gardens, it's not immediately visible and can only be seen at certain angles. This idea can be scaled down; just be sure the garden is wide enough for all the elements. Also keep in mind that you will need plentiful plantings to hide the secret garden from front view. For fun, place the pot on a turntable so its different scenes can unfold in front of you.

## MATERIALS

Planted pot, at least 12 inches across
    (pictured is a 22-inch-diameter
    water bowl drilled for drainage)

Stone sheet, 12 inches by 12 inches

Loose stones for path

Border edging, 12 inches

Wood skewers, 3–5

Dry mini patio mix, 1½ pounds

Dry sand

Moss

Miniature garden accessories

*From this perspective,
no one would suspect the
scene harbors a secret
miniature garden.*

## TOOLS AND SUPPLIES

Gloves (optional)

Hand clippers

Scissors

Water sprayer with a mist setting

## A SECRET GARDEN

**1.**

Start with an existing garden featuring varying heights of dwarf trees, shrubs, and groundcover. Clear an area for the secret garden's patio, toward the back of the pot, an area that will not be visible from the opposite side of the garden. Also clear a small swath where the path will go, keeping the width of the path to scale. Make a bend in the pathway so you can't see through to the back of the pot, or the secret garden, when looking at it from the front.

**2.**

Carve out the patio area in the soil, making a ledge about 1 inch deep. Working from one side to the other, line the edge of the patio area with the border edging material, using the skewers to help keep it in place. Cut the skewers to make 3-inch to 4-inch lengths. Measure and cut the border carefully by cutting off a little bit at a time and putting it back in place and measuring it again. Pin in place with the skewer. Smooth out the soil in the patio area and make it level, about 1 inch deep, leaving enough room for the thickness of your patio material, stones, or tiles.

**3.**

Pour about ¼ inch of sand in the patio area; smooth out into corners. Pour about ½ inch of dry mini patio mix on top of the sand; smooth out into corners.

**4.**
Place the stone sheet on top of the patio area and cut the sheet to fit the space. Cut the stones from the unused sheet to fill in any gaps. (You can tear the stones off the mesh, but sometimes the mesh is fiberglass, so use gloves.) Work from one side to the other and use your jigsaw puzzle skills to figure out the best fit, making sure to leave even gaps between rocks. Make sure the stones are level with each other, level in the pot, and even with the pot's edge.

**5.**
Pour some dry mini patio mix on top of the stones and gently brush this into the crevices and corners. Brush off the excess.

**6.**
Check the level again before you gently mist the patio area, working from one side to the other, stopping just before the water begins to pool up on the surface.

## A SECRET GARDEN

**7.**
Now begin working away from the patio. Using the loose stones, create your stepping-stone path through the garden bed. When you are ready to do the second, smaller patio (not set in mini patio mix), work from one side to the other. There is no border to guide you, but visually create an oval or square-shaped area for the patio. Leave consistent space between stones throughout the patio and pathway.

**8.**
Tear off bits of moss to place between the stones. Make it look natural by poking them in randomly throughout the patio.

**9.**
Once the patio has safely cured, place your accessories on both patios. Remember that it's a secret garden—so let viewers discover the surprise for themselves!

*A secluded path connects one patio to a tiny secret garden terrace.*

# A DRY RIVERBED

A REAL MINIATURE STREAM can require complex setup and maintenance, but a dry riverbed delivers the concept with minimal effort. If your riverbed is in an inground miniature garden, it can also give you an access point to step into your garden for weeding or planting. Whether the riverbed is five inches long in a pot, or five feet long in a garden bed, be sure the boulders, stones, and pebbles are scaled appropriately and match in color. To polish off the look, place a few boulders in the landscape. (When the glaciers receded, they placed boulders randomly in the landscape, too.) As for surrounding flora, look to nature—trees such as hemlock and spruce, as well as smaller shrubs, would often flank a stream.

## MATERIALS

Miniature boulders

Rocks

Pebbles

Miniature logs or stumps

Miniature bridge

## TOOLS AND SUPPLIES

Gloves (optional)

Garden claw or trowel

Kneeler

*A red bridge over a dry streambed tickles the curiosity.*

## A DRY RIVER BED

**1.**

For an established miniature garden, use a trowel or garden fork to gradually carve a river area, about 1 inch to 2 inches in depth. Think about the riverbank and carve right up to plants; avoid creating straight edges and the urge to make it perfect. For a new miniature garden, plant your shortest plants on the edges of the riverbank, with the odd tree added for contrast.

*Fallen logs and large stones are natural to dry streambeds*

**2.**
Place your largest miniature boulders randomly on both sides of the carved area to establish the riverbank. Nestle them in and out of the plants. Position them randomly, with no identifiable pattern. Think about how the water would flow and push big stones into place gradually over time; create inlets with a couple of boulders placed further toward the center of the streambed.

**3.**
Place smaller rocks next to the boulders, nestling them beside the bigger rocks. Set some towards the middle. Again, be random in placement. Your riverbanks should be haphazardly lined with rocks at this point.

**4.**
Add a few small stumps and logs along the edge. Think about how they get caught and trapped on the river's edge. Or perhaps a tree that fell decades ago is now almost decayed, half in the river and half out, overlapping the riverbank.

## A DRY RIVER BED

**5.**
Finish by pouring small pebbles into the bottom of the riverbed. Make sure they cover any soil. Sprinkle them around bigger rocks along the banks of the river. If the scale is large enough, tamp them down by walking on the riverbed.

**6.**
Spray rocks and pebbles with water to wash off any dirt. This also helps to settle the rocks into their new home.

**7.**
It always helps to have some kind of accessory, even when creating a natural or forest scene, to communicate scale to the viewer. Choose an element to suit your theme—a bridge for a trail-like feel, wildlife for a forest theme. Animals can work especially well; tuck them between the bushes at the river's edge. If you include a bridge, don't forget paths at each end for when you're on mental hikes. (Always tell someone where you are going and bring a fully charged cell phone.)

*Over the river and through the woods.*

# A POND IN A POT

IT'S EASY TO LOVE full-sized ponds and water features—but not the time and money they require. This simple, affordable miniature offers a captivating alternative. The cohesiveness of the scene is enhanced if the pots complement each other in color and texture, but they don't have to match exactly. Investing in high quality pots is a good idea simply because a garden of this size can stay in the pot and grow together for years. Accessorize modestly, or with whimsical additions such as a small frog biding his time on the pond's edge, because the pond is a focal point all to itself.

## MATERIALS

Big pot for entire garden

Smaller pond pot with no drainage hole

Medium-sized plastic plant pots, 2 to 4

Plants of your choice

Small pebbles

Landscape cloth, 12 inches by 12 inches

Potting soil

Accessories

*Water features bring an enticing dimension to miniature gardens.*

## TOOLS AND SUPPLIES

Gloves (optional)

Knife

Pitcher of water

## A POND IN A POT

**1.**

Choose the best place for the pond beforehand; off-center is always more interesting. Figure out the level of the pond in the bigger pot by stacking a couple of plastic plant pots upside down in the bottom of the garden container. The number of plastic pots you'll need will depend on the depth of your big pot. Place your pond pot on top of the stack. This precarious platform will eventually be surrounded by soil on all sides to keep it safely upright. The level of the pond pot should be about 1 inch higher than the edge of the big pot—so you can visually sit down on the pond's edge. Play around with the stack of pots—add, take away, or cut off whatever you need to get the pond pot to the right height.

**2.**

Pour in soil around the plastic pot stack, making sure there are no air pockets. Fill up the area with soil and begin planting your garden.

**3.**

Place taller trees in the back and tier down with shorter plants, finishing off with the lowest plants as you work toward the pond area.

**4.**
Finish planting and establish the garden bed edges. Prepare the patio space by clearing an area about ½ inch deep. Tamp down to get rid of any air pockets.

**5.**
Line the bottom of the patio area with landscape cloth, which will keep the pebbles clean longer. In this project, because there are minimal garden edges, the liner acts as the border between the soil and pebbles, so no border edging is needed. Pour small pebbles into the patio an inch below the pond's edge. Tamp down with a flat hand so that the patio surface is level with the garden bed surrounding the rest of the pond pot. Nestle any stepping-stones into the pebbles.

**6.**
Pour clean, clear water into the pond.

## A POND IN A POT

**7.**
Add miniature accessories to set off your new pond focal point.

### Plugging an Existing Hole in Your Pond Pot

**MATERIALS**

A cork

Silicone glue

A stick or skewer

1. The pot and cork should be bone-dry.
2. Carve the cork down so it can fit into the drainage hole. Cut it so it fits the depth of the hole without sticking out the top or the bottom.
3. Spread glue all around the hole with the skewer.
4. Place the cork in the hole.
5. Glue all around the cork on the inside and outside of the pot.
6. Let dry overnight.
7. If the glue dripped while drying, shave off the blobs, making sure you don't break the seal near the hole.
8. Test your new pond with water. If it leaks, pour the water out and let it dry completely. Apply more silicone glue. Let it dry overnight. Test again.

*A pond-side seat offers cool relief on a hot day.*

# A LAKESIDE HIDEAWAY

HAVING A PRIVATE LAKE is the pinnacle of luxury for some people—now you can have your very own to enjoy at your leisure. Tell your friends, family, or co-workers that you just acquired lakefront property and watch the free coffee and small favors start to flow. Take the fun even further and invite friends and family to the lake for a barbecue—and don't forget to tell them to bring their swimsuits and a towel.

## *Setting the Stage for Your Lakefront Haven*

The wood box used in this project is made from 8-inch pine boards with a 1-inch plywood bottom. The outside and about 2 inches down the inside wall of the box were painted with a walnut stain. The rest of the inside of the box was left untreated, as some stains taint the soil and harm the roots. Holes were drilled in the bottom for drainage of excess water or rain. Two small slats of 1-inch by 2-inch wood were attached to the bottom of the box to prop it up off the ground so it can drain more efficiently.

Plant your lakefront property starting with the trees anchoring the corners, then fill in to make a backdrop of trees. Fill in the understory with shorter plants, tucking them underneath and in between the trees as you go. You can use boulders, logs, and stumps in the landscape too, to give the garden a sense of permanence.

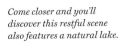

*Come closer and you'll discover this restful scene also features a natural lake.*

## MATERIALS

Wood box with the shoreline planted

Heavy black plastic, 2 feet by 1½ feet

Rock sheet, dark gray

Rocks, an assortment of sizes

Logs, various sizes to match your scale

Moss

Potting soil

Accessories or a toy animal

## TOOLS AND SUPPLIES

Gloves (optional)

Scissors

Pitcher of water

## A LAKESIDE HIDEAWAY

**1.**
With the box already planted, dig out an irregularly shaped area for the lake, about 3 inches to 4 inches deeper than the ground level of your garden. Build up the lakeshore with more soil, remembering to make it a bit irregular to mimic nature.

*Who wouldn't want to dip their toes in these crystal clear waters?*

**2.**
Place the sheet of black plastic over the lake area and hold it in place with a rock on the bottom of the lake. Holding the plastic against the side of the lake with one hand, cut around the shape of the lake, leaving at least 3 inches extra beyond the edge of the lake. Massage the plastic into place as you work around the lake's edge, holding and cutting as you go. With this first cut, leave a generous amount of plastic beyond the rim of the lake—you can always cut more off, but you can't put it back on—and you will eventually hide it with rocks.

**3.**
Pin down the plastic edges with your biggest boulders on all sides. You will have to pleat the plastic in a couple of places; as you massage and work it to fit, it will pleat on its own—just fold it where it wants to go. Create the edges of the lake gradually, filling in with larger rocks followed by progressively smaller stones.

**4.**
Add the odd stump or driftwood logs to your miniature shoreline. Cut off any plastic that is too long or sticks out. Hold it gently, being careful not to undo your rock placement.

## A LAKESIDE HIDEAWAY

**5.**
Fill in the lakebed gradually with an assortment of rocks. Here, we used a stone sheet to speed up the process, by cutting it like a pie and using the triangles to line the bottom and sides of the lakebed. The stone sheet also hides the black plastic on the floor and walls of the lake; important for realism. Conceal the plastic on the shoreline with more rocks, moss, stumps, and logs.

**6.**
Gradually fill in with smaller rocks, covering the black plastic wherever it is still visible. Place a bigger rock or two in the bottom of the lakebed.

**7.**
Fill in the lake with clean, clear water and place your accessories. Get out your water skis and fire up the boat!

*Stones, mini logs, moss, and shrubs give this lakeside an authentic look and feel.*

# A SMALL BUT SWEET TWIG FENCE AND TRELLIS

FENCE BUILDING HAS BEEN a part of the gardener's life for as long as there have been gardens. Regardless of size or scale, wood fences add order, definition, and a rustic charm to the gardens they surround. What's more, with a little ingenuity, you can use the joining techniques explained here to make your own garden accessories. Utilize different types and textures of twigs to promote the theme. For example, in this project, the fence and trellis are to be placed in a country-formal pot, so we chose twigs from a red twig dogwood for a more polished look. This project is in one-inch scale. (To make the fence and trellis in half-inch scale, divide these measurements in half—and half again to make them in quarter-inch scale.)

### FENCE MATERIALS

Twigs of various thicknesses and
    lengths
Floral wire
Metal rod

### TRELLIS MATERIALS

1 Y twig, 8 inches long
3 smaller twigs, 4 inches, 5 inches, and
    6 inches long
Floral wire
Metal rod

### FENCE AND TRELLIS
### TOOLS AND SUPPLIES

Clippers
Wire cutters
Flat-nosed pliers
Box knife
Ruler
Drill

*Gardening under the
shade of an elm tree.*

TWIG FENCE

## *Twigology 101*

Not all branches are created equal. Choose twigs from trees and shrubs for the most part, as stalks from perennials can become brittle once dried. Some tree and shrub twigs have a soft center and you may not need to drill—just poke a rod into the center to make it stand up in the soil.

Twigs clipped directly from trees or shrubs can be used right away, but they get sturdier when dried for a couple of weeks before using. If you do work with freshly harvested twigs, you will have to go back and tighten the wire joints after the twigs dry out and shrink.

However, only fresh twigs bend easily and are preferred for designs that require shaping or curved lines. Bend slowly at first to test the limits of the branch; you are pulling apart the wood fibers and ultimately compromising the integrity of the wood. Pin, brace, or tie the branch to keep the curve in place while the branch dries out for a few days. When you remove the binding, the branch will stay curved.

**1.**
Cut two fence posts from the thicker branch, each about 4 inches long. Cut the top of the post at a slant (they do this with full-sized fencing so the rain runs off). The cut at the bottom of the post should be straight.

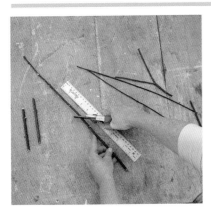

**2.**
From skinnier twigs, cut two 8-inch-long pieces for the rails of the fence. The ends can be cut at an angle or straight, your choice.

**3.**
Put the fence together on the table and, while holding the piece in place with one hand, score each post on both sides of the rail with the box knife, exactly where you are going to join it. Do this at all intersections where the posts and rails meet.

**4.**
Cut into the scores with the box knife, about 1/16 inch deep, and whittle out a notch. Do this for the other three spots where you scored the posts. It's not imperative to notch the twigs to wire them together, but the pieces will last a lot longer out in the elements when they are notched before joining.

## TWIG FENCE

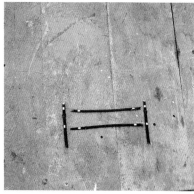

**5.**

Flip the fence over and place the posts and rails together again. Score the rail on both sides of the post at all intersections. Make sure the rails are lined up evenly with each other.

**6.**

Cut into the incision about $\frac{1}{16}$ inch; whittle out the notch. When you are done, you should have a total of eight notches, two on each twig.

**7.**

Cut four pieces of wire, each about 3 inches long, and bend each into a U shape. Holding the rail and post, notches together, place the U above the rail and bend the wire around the post and to the back of the fence.

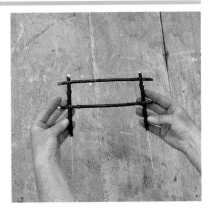

**8.**
Twist the wire together on the back side of the post; tighten with pliers. Cut excess wire ends with wire cutters. Bend the wire ends up or down so you won't get poked when placing the fence in the miniature garden.

**9.**
Drill a hole in the bottom of a post. Repeat on other posts. Glue rods in holes with two-part epoxy.

**10.**
A secure section of miniature fencing, waiting for placement in the garden.

## TWIG TRELLIS

**1.**
Using the Y twig as a guide, cut three crosspieces for the trellis, approximately 4 inches, 5 inches, and 6 inches long. Lay the pieces together on the table to be sure you have the right sizes and design.

**2.**
Cut six pieces of wire, each about 2½ inches long and bend them in a U. Holding the trellis together with one of the crosspieces, place the U above the crosspiece and bend the wire around the other twig and to the back of the fence. Twist the wire together on the back side so it's tight enough to stay put; you'll tighten all the joints when the crosspieces are in place.

**3.**
Work through the remaining joints, doing one crosspiece at a time.

*A miniature trellis is perfect for training a dwarf clematis.*

## TWIG TRELLIS

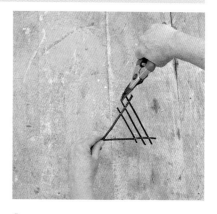

**4.**
Adjust the alignment of the railings and post to make sure the trellis is square and parallel. Tighten all the wire joints with the flat-nosed pliers so they are just snug. Be careful not to twist too much, or you'll twist the wire into the twig and break it.

**5.**
Clip off excess wire and fold the end in so it doesn't poke you when you position it in your miniature garden.

**6.**
Trim the ends of the crosspieces to even them up.

**7.**
Drill the end of the Y and glue a rod in it.

**8.**
A miniature trellis, ready for placement in your garden.

# YOUR FORK
# AS A RAKE

## MINIATURE GARDEN
## MAINTENANCE

EVERY GARDEN requires some ongoing attention. Whether it's a tiny landscape sitting
on your desk at work or an inground miniature empire in your front yard, plants need
regular care. Hopefully, you have chosen
a size and type of small-scale garden that
corresponds with your lifestyle and desired
involvement. It really is your own project to
build and grow however you like.

*Caring for miniature gardens can require as little
as a few minutes a month.*

Miniature gardening tasks range from routine watering to dividing plants once a year, but unlike what often happens with full-sized gardening, you shouldn't ever feel overwhelmed. Remember that we are combining crafting with gardening—the craft fun is in the conception and building, the gardening is in the planting, growing, and maintenance. While basic requirements are similar to those for larger gardens, maintaining a miniature garden can take as little as a few minutes a month, not including time spent watering. In this chapter we'll cover what it takes to keep your miniature garden thriving for years to come.

## WATERING YOUR MINIATURE WORLD

For the new gardener, knowing when to water is often daunting, but it doesn't have to be. The main considerations are where the miniature garden is planted and how much water the plants need. Remember that when you were planning your garden, you chose plants with the same general watering requirements, which will simplify things.

New plants take a while to grow root hairs into the soil. These tiny tendrils soak up moisture and allow the plant to go for periods without water. Larger roots anchor and hold the plant in place. Water inground gardens attentively for the first year to help plants adjust to their new home. Avoid overwatering by sticking your finger one inch into the soil and testing the level of dampness. Water deeply and infrequently to train the roots to look for their own water. Planting your outdoor miniature garden in spring or fall is the ideal time, as rain will help with the watering; however, don't rely on rainfall to supply all of your garden's watering needs. Checking with your finger is always the best gauge. After the first year, inground plants require less attention, but will still need a little watering in the dry months.

*The garden may be miniature, but the tools of the trade are standard size.*

Watering container gardens is more precise but not difficult. It is easy to overwater if you aren't careful; roots need air to breathe and water-logged soil chokes out air. On the other hand, containers dry out quickly in hot summer months. Some plants can survive being parched but for the most part they have a hard time recovering from lack of water.

Think of the container garden as a small eco-system where the plants are limited in their search for food and water, so they rely on you to fulfill those needs. If you are a new gardener, keep a close eye on your containers, especially during dry periods, and use the finger test to monitor soil moisture.

All containers should have a drainage hole or two, depending on the size of the container. Stones in the bottom of the pot are not necessary, although some gardeners insist that they help with drainage. However, the space they take up could be filled with extra soil, which is ultimately what roots need. When watering, give your container garden a deep, thorough soak until water drains from the holes in the bottom. Repeat this as needed, depending on the temperature and your plants' particular needs, using the finger check to see if more or less watering is needed.

Note that plants will need more water during their growing periods in spring and summer, and less during the dormant months of fall and winter. For outdoor garden plants, it is critical that the soil

*Illusion in the miniature garden is equal parts art, craft, and maintenance.*

remain damp throughout the freezing months of winter, whether plants are in the ground or in a pot. Roots can tolerate the soil freezing around their roots, but they won't tolerate being freeze-dried. If the soil feels dry during the winter, or if you are expecting a freeze, water with cold water.

Always water your miniature garden gently from the back of the planter. Late afternoons or early mornings are the best times to do this, so the heat of the day will not evaporate the water and your effort. If water gets on the miniature patio, wait until it dries, then sweep up any soil that may have washed onto the stone, using your fingers or a dry paintbrush as a broom.

If you're worried that you'll forget to water, pick a day of the week and mark the same day on your calendar for the next six months. Then check your plant's soil moisture every week on that day, and water if necessary. Eventually, watering will become second nature. After a while, you will learn how to tell exactly when your plants need water, and will not need a schedule anymore.

While it's easier to use plants with the same water needs, you can mix moisture-loving plants with dry-loving plants in the same container. Plant the water-loving plant in its own pot, then plant that pot in the larger garden container. That will separate the water for the moisture-loving plant from the soil in the rest of the garden, and you can water it more often. For inground miniature gardens, this trick has mixed results, as plants are all subject to the same weather and it's harder to keep soil moisture levels separate.

LEFT: *Check soil moisture often to avoid watering too much or too little.*

BELOW: *Sawara-cypress, 'Tom Thumb' cotoneaster, and 'Jean's Dilly' dwarf spruce have the same water needs, which streamlines maintenance.*

RIGHT: *Tending to a conifer's water needs will keep its needles green and supple.*

## GIVE IT SOME AIR

Whether in containers or outside in beds, soil should be aerated to keep it from compacting. This helps growth-enhancing air and water get through to the roots—and the roots to get through the soil. With the constant watering and drying out that happens in containers, the soil will eventually form a crusty layer and ridges will form, directing the water down the sides of the pot, away from the plant's roots. So aerate every few weeks, using an old kitchen fork, small rod, or stick to poke down a few inches between plants, while lightly churning the surface soil. For inground gardens, use a hoe, rake, or a garden claw to break up this crusty layer. Your plants will thank you.

## FEEDING TIME

As mentioned, fertilizing your miniature garden is not high on the list of priorities because you don't want plants to grow too quickly. The objective is to keep your wee world together for as long as possible (or not, depending upon your taste for change). Instead of fertilizing, some gardeners mulch with manure and compost, which breaks down and feeds the soil. Fresh potting soil is infused with nutrients, but after a couple of years, a light application of a timed-release organic fertilizer is a good idea for containers. Less is always better than more. Follow directions carefully.

Some plants also have specific feeding preferences. Annuals like a couple of feedings throughout the growing months, and perennials respond well to fertilizer in the spring and the first half of the summer. Most potted conifers do not require fertilizer at all for the first couple of years, then need a little timed-release fertilizer during the growing season. Inground conifers do not need any fertilizer.

*Keeping the soil in your miniature yard aerated will help plants thrive.*

# MAINTAINING GROUNDCOVERS

Groundcovers grow in various ways. By taking note of these growth habits, you can control the plant's reach and extend the life of your miniature garden.

Some groundcovers spread across the top of the ground by extending a branch and sending roots down into the soil from that branch. Vines typically spread this way, as do Scottish and Irish moss. By clipping or pinching this new growth, you can slow its spread with minimal fuss.

Other groundcovers send shoots out from the main plant just below the surface or up to an inch deep, where the runner (the shoot growing under the soil) sends up leaves. These leaves access the light and allow the plant to continue growing. You can borrow a technique from railroad gardeners and shovel-prune around the plant, severing the new growth, then tug at the above-ground ends of the runners to pull out the cut stems. Of course, you wouldn't take a big spade to your small garden; you can use a grapefruit spoon, a sharp chisel, or a pair of heavy-duty scissors to achieve the same result.

Then there are groundcovers that reseed, some more generously than others. Simply pull up the new growth whenever you see it. The more the shoot grows, the more mess you will make removing it, so be sure to pull the unwanted seedling as soon as you see it.

*Fill in bare spots with ground-hugging plants.*

## DIVIDE AND REPLANT

If you are gardening in a container, you may have to divide groundcovers every couple of years. This sounds a lot worse than it actually is, and takes less time than you might think. From the back of the garden, using a trowel, gently slip the blade down along the back side of the pot. Using leverage from the trowel—don't use the pot's edge, or it may break—gently lift up and loosen the plant's roots a bit. Take the trowel out and do the same thing on the other sides of the plant. You are essentially cutting the plant out of the pot. When all sides are loosened, using your hands, gently lift up the clump of groundcover out of the pot. Divide it gently by pulling it apart as you would a soft dinner roll: gently but firmly. Put the more desirable clump back in the miniature garden and make sure to face the nicest side of the plant toward the garden's front.

The roots of your plants will eventually outgrow their pot. This will take several seasons, depending on the size of the pot and the plants you have used. With either an old kitchen knife or a trowel, cut down along the interior sides of the pot—just as when you free the sides of a cake from its baking pan. This will cut any roots that have stuck to the sides of the pot. Then tip the garden pot on its side and hold it in place with one hand, while coaxing the contents out of the pot with your other hand. When the garden is out of the pot, start separating out the plants that will be moving to another home, coaxing the roots apart gently. You can use divided plants to make another garden, plant them in an inground bed, or give them to a fellow miniature gardener.

You can also prune roots by taking the plant out of the pot and cutting the roots by no more than one-third, and replacing the plant in the pot with some fresh potting soil. Water thoroughly.

*Sedum spurium 'Tricolor' sends out leggy branches that will root and slowly turn into a dividable new plant.*

## PRUNE IF NECESSARY

The urge to prune a miniature garden is often strong. A snip here, a snip there on a sunny summer morning is heaven on earth to some people. In this type of gardening, however, you prune sparingly rather than as a routine practice, because it only encourages more growth.

The frequency and type of pruning can vary depending upon your plants, but there are some general rules. For all plants, prune any dead, dying, broken, or diseased branches, and branches that are rubbing or crossing each other. For most plants, prune after the spring growth spurt or after they finish flowering. For perennials, deadhead spent flowers to get the plants to bloom again before they go to seed. If the plant is getting leggy, meaning all the growth is at the top of the stems, and you see new growth at the base of the groundcover or perennial, prune the stems to just above the new buds—this will direct the plant's energy to the young growth.

To help a plant keep its shape, or to direct the branches where you want them to go, prune or pinch back just above a set of leaves, and remove no more than one-third of the plant at a time to give it a chance to recover. Trimming too much of the plant at once may kill it.

*Only prune miniature plants when you must, to help them keep their shape and place.*

# PLANTING TIMES FOR OUTDOOR GARDENS

Indoor container planting, fortunately, can be done anytime. But planting outdoors requires a little more planning and attention.

For inground gardens, fall is the best time to plant. New plants will get watering help with autumn rains and will go dormant along with the rest of the garden come wintertime. When spring arrives, the roots will be established and stable. Monitor new plantings for the first full summer to make sure they get the water they need. By the second summer they will be established and only need water in extreme drought conditions.

If you are in a temperate zone and the ground is not frozen, you can also plant in the winter. If the weather has been very wet, hold off until the soil dries out a bit. Working the ground when it is soaked will harm the tiny microcosms and air pockets that are needed for healthy soil.

Springtime is another good time to plant, as spring rains nurture new transplants. Again, if the soil is waterlogged, let it dry out before you dig. If the ground is frozen, wait for it to thaw completely. If it is a dry spring, you will have to provide the water. Generally, plants take a season or two to become established, so you will still have to tend your miniature garden closely through the first summer. You may want to add some compost or peat moss to the soil before planting, to help it retain moisture.

In more temperate regions, you can plant in summer, but in the hotter climates, fall is better for inground planting. With excessive heat and full sun, plants may not survive both transplant shock and extreme hot weather. The roots are not yet established, so maintain a regular watering schedule for the rest of the summer. Shade new plants that are in extreme heat and sun. A big golf or garden umbrella works well. Anchor the end of the umbrella, or use tent stakes and rope to hold it in place.

Trees are especially vulnerable to transplant shock and weather conditions, so if you can, plant them in the fall or spring. If you must plant a tree in the summer, some special care will increase your chance of success. After digging the hole for planting, fill it with water and let it drain. Add a bit of timed-release fertilizer for a little boost. While holding the plant suspended inside the planting hole with one hand, use your other hand to scoop the soil back into the hole, around the roots. Spread out your fingers and gently push the soil through and to the root ball to engage the roots with the new soil. Water thoroughly and deeply. Turn down the hose until the water is trickling out and place the end of the hose at the base of the newly planted tree to soak the soil for a few minutes to half an hour.

*To turn a shrub into a tree, trim the bottom-most branches to show more of the trunk and lower branches.*

## CONIFER DIEBACK

LEFT: *Garden or golf umbrellas can help shield new plantings from periods of extreme summer sun.*

RIGHT: *Check conifers for conifer dieback, which can block the plant's light and air.*

Conifers, like all evergreens, lose needles throughout the year. This is called conifer dieback. Many dwarf conifers hold the dead foliage in their branches, which prevents light and air from reaching the center of the plant. This is particularly troublesome for very tight-growing types and can kill individual branches—and eventually the entire plant—if dropped debris is not cleared away.

To check your conifer for dieback, part the branches to view its center (gloves are advised). Stick your fingers through the branches into the center of the tree, and slough off any dead foliage. You can use a garden fork as a rake to clean up the debris. If you're working in a pot that has been growing for at least a year, you can carefully tip the entire pot over onto its side, and brush off the dead needles. Sprinkle some timed-release fertilizer on top of the container, give the outside of the pot a good wipe with a damp cloth, and the garden is ready for summer!

Check for conifer dieback every season. Some miniature and dwarf conifers shed from the middle of autumn right through to late summer. If you check often and early, you can easily stay on top of this necessary chore.

LEFT: *Planted in the spring, this pink-flowering sea thrift is ready to bloom, come summer.*

RIGHT: *Outdoor container gardens can be planted anytime.*

## POTTING FORWARD

As you get further into this wonderful hobby, the trees will grow up slowly, your groundcovers will spread, and you'll find that your miniature garden keeps getting more and more magical. It really becomes an old friend after a number of years.

But there will come a time when you'll need to pull a tree out because it has grown too large for the scale of the garden, the soil level has gone down in the pot, or you are simply in need of a change. You may want to keep the garden in its pot and just give it a makeover. You may also want to transfer the tree to an inground bed and start a brand new miniature garden. Most important, you'll have options galore, having learned how to grow your own world.

*It takes decades for some miniature gardens to grow into their full glory.*

*When a miniature tree outgrows its container, look for a place it can fit into an outdoor bed.*

*Count on a fairy house to
add a hint of magic to your
miniature garden.*

# ADDITIONAL READING

**To complement your miniature garden adventures, I've included a list of books you may enjoy, along with notes about why I like the book.**

Ashberry, Anne. 1951. *Miniature Gardens*. London: C. Arthur Pearson, Limited. One of the few books on miniature gardening that focus on the hobby. It is full of plant information. Anne wrote several other books about miniature plants that are interesting to the hard-core miniature gardener.

Bloom, Adrian. 2002. *Gardening With Conifers*. Richmond Hill / Buffalo: Firefly Books. A gorgeous book that gives an overview of conifers, with references to the miniature and dwarf conifers we love for miniature gardening. Ultimate height of each conifer listed is included.

Brickell, Christopher, and H. Marc Cathey. 2004. *The American Horticultural Society A-Z Encyclopedia of Garden Plants*. New York: DK Publishing. An indispensable plant reference for the garden. Includes heat zone information that the southern states and warmer regions will find very useful.

Constable, John. 1984. *Landscapes in Miniature*. London: Lutterworth Press (Guildford) and Sheldon Press (London). Very detailed and project oriented. May be of more interest to the miniaturist than to the gardener.

Edwards Forkner, Lorene. 2011. *Handmade Garden Projects*. Portland: Timber Press. Lorene has a lovely how-to in here on creating your own miniature knot garden made out of boxwood cuttings.

Fincham, Robert L. 2011. *Small Conifers for Small Gardens*. Eatonville: Coenosium Press. An interesting read for conifer lovers. Robert has included a short history of each plant listed.

Gray, Freida. 1999. *Making Miniature Gardens*. East Sussex: Guild of Master Craftsman Publications Ltd. Focuses on creating artificial miniature gardens. Some of the projects can be used for living miniature gardens.

Hessayon, Dr. D. G. 2002. *The Houseplant Expert*. New York: Expert Books. A great reference for indoor plants.

Moorey, Teresa. 2008. *The Fairy Bible: the Definitive Guide to the World of Fairies*. New York: Sterling Publishing Company. A very cute and very complete reference to everything fairy.

Schenk, George. 2006. *Gardening on Pavement, Tables, and Hard Surfaces*. Portland: Timber Press. A fun book full of gorgeous ideas. You'll learn that you don't need as much space for a plant's roots as you think you do.

Tajima, Lisa. 2004. *Pop Bonsai*. New York: Kodansha International. A very fun book that will inspire you to be even more creative with tiny plants.

# METRIC CONVERSIONS

| INCHES | CENTIMETERS |
|--------|-------------|
| ¼ | 0.6 |
| ½ | 1.3 |
| ¾ | 1.9 |
| 1 | 2.5 |
| 2 | 5.1 |
| 3 | 7.6 |
| 4 | 10 |
| 5 | 13 |
| 6 | 15 |
| 7 | 18 |
| 8 | 20 |
| 9 | 23 |
| 10 | 25 |

| FEET | METERS |
|------|--------|
| 1 | 0.3 |
| 2 | 0.6 |
| 3 | 0.9 |
| 4 | 1.2 |
| 5 | 1.5 |
| 6 | 1.8 |
| 7 | 2.1 |
| 8 | 2.4 |
| 9 | 2.7 |
| 10 | 3 |
| 20 | 6 |
| 30 | 9 |
| 40 | 12 |

**TEMPERATURES**

$°C = \frac{5}{9} \times (°F - 32)$

$°F = (\frac{9}{5} \times °C) + 32$

**FLUID VOLUME MEASUREMENTS**

| | |
|--------|--------|
| 1 ounce | 30 mL |
| 4 ounces | 125 mL |
| 8 ounces | 250 mL |
| 12 ounces | 375 mL |
| 16 ounces | 500 mL |
| 1 pint | 500 mL |
| 1 quart | 1 L |
| 1 gallon | 4 L |

# ACKNOWLEDGMENTS

This path on which I have found myself was paved by many people who nudged and helped me along the way. Starting at the beginning of my journey, I would like to thank Maria Ruano of Bedrock Industries for turning my efforts toward the garden industry many moons ago; it was a pivotal step in this long journey. I would like to thank Kristine Hill, of the Seattle Dollhouse Miniature Show, for her undying enthusiasm and support of the miniature side of my passion. One can never get too many Best of Show ribbons to feel validated and motivated to stay focused; they still hang in my office. A belated thank-you to the late Joyce Clifford of Dolly's Dollhouse, for fostering the startup of my business; I was able to expand and share the joy of miniatures with the world through my online store. A warm thank-you to Carol Nehring of Iseli Nursery, who took me under her wing and tolerated my tiny tree orders and detailed requests in the midst of a huge nursery operation—I couldn't have done it without your help.

Thank you, Barbara Peterman, for without your giant nudge and professional advice, this book would still be in pieces on my shelf. Your way of directing my writing was so thoughtful and subtle, I didn't even realize you were doing it until months afterward. A huge thank-you to all my friends and family, for understanding that I had to drop off the face of the earth to get this done. Thank you, Mom, for your never-ending support as always, and for proofing every word of this book with your expert eye—twice.

There are no words in the dictionary for the amount of gratitude I have for my loving husband, Steve. Thank you for coming over to the "green side" and moving mountains with me. You took over the house, the online store operation, and pretty much held down every aspect of our lives while I pushed this out the door. And all of that on top of being my biggest fan. You are my rock.

The biggest and warmest thank-you goes to all my fellow miniature gardeners throughout the world—you were with me every step of the way. Each and every time it got too rough, and I was ready to pack it all in, I would get an e-mail, phone call, or a card to thank me for inspiring you. Those very timely injections of encouragement and positive energy made me sit right down and get back to work. This book is for you.

## PHOTO CREDITS

Photos by Kate Baldwin appear on pages 8–9, 11, 14, 15, 17, 20–21, 23, 31, 33, 38, 39, 40, 41, 43, 44, 45, 46 right, 48–49, 50, 53, 54, 57 right, 58, 59, 60, 61, 63, 64–65, 66–67, 69, 70–71, 72, 77, 80–81, 83, 84–85, 88, 89, 91 right, 93, 95, 96, 102–103, 104, 105 left, 108–109, 111, 112, 113, 115, 120, 121, 123, 125, 126, 128 left, 130, 133, 134, 135, 137, 138–139, 142, 144, 146–147, 149, 150, 153, 154–155, 160, 161, 162, 163, 164, 165, 166, 168–169, 170, 172–219, 220–221, 223, 224–225, 227, 230–231, 234–235, 241, 242–243, 245

All other photographs are by Janit Calvo.

# INDEX